Sonja Eggerickx

Leading Belgium's LGBTQ Education Revolution – Unfiltered

Ibrahim Pereira

ISBN: 9781779697059
Imprint: Telephasic Workshop
Copyright © 2024 Ibrahim Pereira.
All Rights Reserved.

Contents

Introduction

The power of activism

Creating change through education and awareness

Education is a powerful tool for social change, particularly in the realm of LGBTQ rights. It fosters understanding, empathy, and acceptance, which are crucial for dismantling prejudice and discrimination. Through education, we can challenge harmful stereotypes and provide individuals with the knowledge necessary to advocate for themselves and others. This section explores how Sonja Eggerickx harnessed the power of education and awareness to create tangible change for the LGBTQ community in Belgium.

Theoretical Framework

The foundation of educational activism can be understood through various theoretical lenses. One such lens is Paulo Freire's *Pedagogy of the Oppressed*, which emphasizes the importance of critical consciousness. Freire argues that education should not merely be a transfer of knowledge but a practice of freedom that empowers individuals to question and challenge the status quo. This approach aligns with LGBTQ activism, as it encourages marginalized individuals to articulate their experiences and advocate for their rights.

Another relevant theory is the *Social Learning Theory* proposed by Albert Bandura, which posits that individuals learn behaviors and norms through observation and imitation. By integrating LGBTQ topics into educational curricula, students can observe positive representations of LGBTQ individuals, which can foster acceptance and reduce stigma. This theory underscores the importance of visibility and representation in education.

Identifying Problems

The lack of LGBTQ-inclusive education in Belgium has historically contributed to a culture of ignorance and intolerance. Many schools have failed to provide accurate information about LGBTQ identities, leading to misconceptions and negative attitudes. For example, a 2019 study by the Belgian LGBTQ organization *Çavaria* revealed that 60% of LGBTQ students reported feeling unsafe at school due to their sexual orientation or gender identity. This alarming statistic highlights the urgent need for educational reform.

Moreover, the absence of LGBTQ representation in educational materials perpetuates the idea that LGBTQ identities are deviant or abnormal. This not only affects LGBTQ students but also reinforces harmful stereotypes among their heterosexual peers. As a result, the cycle of discrimination continues, impacting the mental health and well-being of LGBTQ youth.

Examples of Change

Sonja Eggerickx recognized these issues and took action to create change through education. One of her significant initiatives was the establishment of the LGBTQ Education Foundation, which aimed to develop comprehensive educational resources that included LGBTQ topics. This foundation collaborated with educators to create curricula that not only addressed LGBTQ history and issues but also promoted inclusive practices within schools.

For instance, the foundation developed a program called *Safe Spaces*, which trained teachers on how to create inclusive classrooms. This program emphasized the importance of using inclusive language, addressing bullying, and providing support for LGBTQ students. By equipping educators with the tools they needed, Sonja's initiative fostered a more accepting environment for all students.

Another example of change is the implementation of LGBTQ-inclusive sex education in schools. Traditional sex education often neglects LGBTQ perspectives, leaving many students without essential information about their identities. By advocating for inclusive curricula, Sonja helped ensure that LGBTQ youth received accurate and relevant information about their health and relationships.

The Ripple Effect

The impact of education extends beyond the classroom. When students learn about LGBTQ issues and develop empathy for their peers, they are more likely to become allies and advocates for change. This ripple effect can lead to a more inclusive society, where individuals feel empowered to stand up against discrimination and support LGBTQ rights.

Research has shown that inclusive education can significantly reduce instances of bullying and violence against LGBTQ individuals. A study published in the *Journal of School Health* found that schools with LGBTQ-inclusive curricula reported a 30% decrease in bullying incidents related to sexual orientation and gender identity. This statistic underscores the transformative power of education in creating safer environments for LGBTQ youth.

In conclusion, creating change through education and awareness is a vital aspect of LGBTQ activism. By addressing the gaps in LGBTQ-inclusive education, Sonja Eggerickx has played a crucial role in fostering understanding, acceptance, and advocacy within Belgian society. Through her efforts, she has not only empowered LGBTQ youth but has also paved the way for future generations to continue the fight for equality and justice.

The importance of LGBTQ rights

The importance of LGBTQ rights transcends mere legal recognition; it encompasses the fundamental principles of human dignity, equality, and respect. In a world where diversity is a natural human condition, the acknowledgment and protection of LGBTQ rights are essential for fostering inclusive societies that celebrate rather than marginalize differences.

Human Rights Framework

At the core of LGBTQ rights is the assertion that every individual, regardless of their sexual orientation or gender identity, possesses inherent rights as articulated in international human rights frameworks. The Universal Declaration of Human Rights (UDHR), adopted by the United Nations in 1948, states in Article 1 that "All human beings are born free and equal in dignity and rights." This principle extends to LGBTQ individuals, who have historically been subjected to discrimination, violence, and systemic exclusion.

The Yogyakarta Principles, developed in 2006, further elaborate on the application of international human rights law in relation to sexual orientation and gender identity. These principles emphasize that states must ensure the protection of LGBTQ individuals from discrimination and violence, affirming that such rights are not optional but fundamental to human rights.

Social and Economic Implications

The lack of recognition of LGBTQ rights has profound social and economic implications. Discrimination against LGBTQ individuals can lead to severe mental health issues, including depression and anxiety, which are exacerbated by societal stigma. According to a study by the Williams Institute, LGBTQ youth are more than twice as likely to experience bullying and harassment in schools compared to their heterosexual peers. This environment not only affects their educational performance but also their future economic opportunities.

The economic costs of discrimination are substantial. A 2019 report from the McKinsey Global Institute found that advancing LGBTQ equality could contribute $3.7 trillion to the global economy. By creating inclusive workplaces and communities, societies can harness the full potential of all their members, leading to innovation, productivity, and growth.

Cultural Representation and Visibility

Cultural representation plays a critical role in the recognition of LGBTQ rights. Visibility in media, literature, and public life helps to normalize diverse identities and experiences. The portrayal of LGBTQ characters in films and television has increased dramatically in recent years, providing positive role models and fostering empathy among audiences. For example, the success of films like *Moonlight* and *Call Me by Your Name* has not only highlighted LGBTQ narratives but also contributed to broader discussions about acceptance and love.

However, representation is not merely about visibility; it is about authenticity. The importance of telling stories that reflect the lived experiences of LGBTQ individuals cannot be overstated. When marginalized voices are elevated, it challenges stereotypes and dismantles prejudices, paving the way for greater acceptance and understanding.

Legal Protections and Policy Changes

Legal protections for LGBTQ individuals are crucial for safeguarding their rights. Countries that have implemented anti-discrimination laws and policies demonstrate a commitment to equality. For instance, Belgium's legalization of same-sex marriage in 2003 marked a significant milestone in the fight for LGBTQ rights, setting a precedent for other nations.

Moreover, comprehensive anti-discrimination laws that encompass employment, housing, and public accommodations are essential to protect LGBTQ individuals from bias. The Equality Act in the United States, which aims to prohibit discrimination based on sexual orientation and gender identity, is a pivotal example of legislative efforts to secure equal rights for LGBTQ individuals.

Intersectionality in LGBTQ Rights

It is essential to approach LGBTQ rights through an intersectional lens, recognizing that individuals experience oppression in multiple forms. Factors such as race, ethnicity, socioeconomic status, and disability intersect with sexual orientation and gender identity, creating unique challenges. For example, LGBTQ people of color often face compounded discrimination, leading to higher rates of violence and marginalization within both the LGBTQ community and society at large.

Addressing these intersectional issues requires a holistic approach to activism and policy-making, ensuring that the voices of the most marginalized within the LGBTQ community are heard and prioritized.

The Ongoing Struggle for Equality

Despite significant progress, the struggle for LGBTQ rights is far from over. In many parts of the world, LGBTQ individuals still face criminalization, violence, and persecution. For instance, in countries where homosexuality is illegal, individuals can face imprisonment or even death. The global landscape of LGBTQ rights remains uneven, with some nations making strides while others regress.

Activism remains a vital force in advocating for change. Grassroots movements, such as Pride marches and campaigns for legal reforms, play an essential role in raising awareness and mobilizing support. The ongoing fight for LGBTQ rights is not just a matter of legal recognition but a quest for societal acceptance and understanding.

Conclusion

In conclusion, the importance of LGBTQ rights lies in their fundamental connection to human dignity, equality, and social justice. As societies continue to evolve, the recognition and protection of these rights will be crucial in building inclusive communities that value diversity. The work of activists like Sonja Eggerickx exemplifies the tireless efforts required to advance LGBTQ rights and create a world where everyone can live authentically and freely.

$$\text{LGBTQ Rights} \rightarrow \text{Human Dignity} + \text{Social Justice} + \text{Economic Growth} \quad (1)$$

Sonja Eggerickx: A trailblazer for LGBTQ education in Belgium

Sonja Eggerickx stands as a pivotal figure in the landscape of LGBTQ education in Belgium, a country that has made significant strides in the recognition of LGBTQ rights but still grapples with the complexities of inclusive education. Her journey is not merely a personal narrative but a reflection of a broader societal transformation. The importance of her work can be understood through the lens of educational theory, social justice, and the ongoing struggle against discrimination.

Theoretical Framework

At the core of Sonja's activism is the concept of *social justice education*, which emphasizes the need for an equitable educational environment that recognizes and affirms diverse identities. According to [?], social justice education seeks to address the systemic inequalities faced by marginalized groups, including LGBTQ individuals. This theory is essential in understanding the necessity of LGBTQ-inclusive curricula, which not only validate the experiences of LGBTQ youth but also foster a culture of acceptance among all students.

Sonja's work aligns with *critical pedagogy*, a framework developed by educators such as [?], who argued for an education that empowers students to challenge oppressive systems. By advocating for LGBTQ education, Sonja aims to dismantle the stigma and discrimination that often permeate educational institutions, thereby creating a more inclusive environment for all students.

Identifying the Problems

Despite Belgium's progressive stance on LGBTQ rights, the lack of comprehensive LGBTQ education in schools remains a significant issue. Research conducted by [?] indicates that many educational institutions lack an inclusive curriculum, which contributes to the marginalization of LGBTQ students. This absence of representation can lead to feelings of isolation and low self-esteem among LGBTQ youth, as they do not see their identities reflected in the educational materials.

Moreover, the impact of bullying and discrimination in schools cannot be overstated. According to a study by [?], LGBTQ students are disproportionately affected by bullying, which can result in severe psychological consequences, including anxiety and depression. Sonja recognized these alarming statistics and understood that education is a powerful tool for change.

Sonja's Mission

In response to these challenges, Sonja Eggerickx founded the *LGBTQ Education Foundation*, a groundbreaking initiative aimed at revolutionizing the educational landscape in Belgium. Her mission was clear: to create safe spaces for LGBTQ students and to develop comprehensive educational resources that would be integrated into school curricula across the country.

One of the foundation's key initiatives was the development of training programs for educators, focusing on LGBTQ inclusivity and sensitivity. By equipping teachers with the necessary tools and knowledge, Sonja aimed to foster an environment where LGBTQ students could thrive. This initiative reflects the principles of *transformative learning*, as outlined by [?], which posits that education should facilitate critical reflection and personal growth.

Examples of Success

Sonja's efforts have led to tangible changes within the Belgian educational system. For example, her collaboration with various schools resulted in the implementation of LGBTQ-inclusive curricula that encompass topics such as gender identity, sexual orientation, and the history of LGBTQ rights. These curricula not only educate students about diversity but also promote empathy and understanding, which are crucial in combating prejudice.

Furthermore, the foundation has organized awareness campaigns and workshops that engage both students and parents, creating a community-wide dialogue about LGBTQ issues. One notable campaign, *"Visibility Matters"*, aimed to highlight the importance of representation in education. Through art installations and student-led discussions, the campaign encouraged participants to reflect on their own biases and the impact of visibility on LGBTQ youth.

Legacy and Impact

Sonja Eggerickx's contributions to LGBTQ education in Belgium extend beyond her immediate initiatives. Her work has inspired a new generation of activists and educators who recognize the importance of inclusive education as a catalyst for social change. The ripple effects of her activism are evident in the growing number of educational institutions that prioritize LGBTQ inclusivity, as well as in the increasing visibility of LGBTQ issues in public discourse.

In conclusion, Sonja Eggerickx is not just a trailblazer for LGBTQ education in Belgium; she is a symbol of resilience and hope for countless individuals who continue to fight for their rights. Her commitment to creating an equitable educational landscape serves as a reminder that education is not merely about imparting knowledge but about fostering understanding, acceptance, and ultimately, love. As we reflect on her legacy, it becomes clear that the journey towards LGBTQ equality is ongoing, and the role of education in this fight is more critical than ever.

Chapter One: Discovering the Activist Within

Childhood in Belgium

Early experiences with discrimination

Growing up in Belgium, Sonja Eggerickx encountered the harsh realities of discrimination at a young age. The societal landscape in which she was raised was not devoid of prejudice; rather, it was imbued with subtle and overt forms of bias that permeated the fabric of everyday life. This section delves into Sonja's formative experiences with discrimination, illustrating the profound impact these events had on her development as an activist.

Discrimination can manifest in various forms, including but not limited to verbal harassment, social exclusion, and systemic inequalities. According to the *Social Identity Theory*, individuals categorize themselves and others into groups, which can lead to in-group favoritism and out-group discrimination (Tajfel & Turner, 1979). For Sonja, the intersection of her identity as a young LGBTQ individual with the prevailing societal norms created a challenging environment that often rendered her vulnerable to discriminatory behaviors.

Verbal Harassment Sonja's early experiences were punctuated by instances of verbal harassment. In school, she often faced derogatory remarks from peers, which were rooted in ignorance and fear of the unknown. Such comments, while seemingly innocuous to some, carried a weight that could not be underestimated. Research indicates that verbal harassment can lead to long-term psychological effects, including anxiety and depression (Hatzenbuehler, 2009). Sonja vividly recalls one incident where a classmate mockingly questioned her choice of clothing, insinuating that it was 'too boyish.' This moment, trivialized by many, was a painful reminder of her difference, pushing her further into the recesses of self-doubt.

Social Exclusion   Social exclusion was another painful aspect of Sonja's early life. As she began to express her identity, she found herself increasingly isolated from her peers. The fear of being ostracized loomed large, and her attempts to connect with others were often met with cold shoulders. The concept of *minority stress* (Meyer, 2003) posits that individuals from marginalized groups experience chronic stress due to their stigmatized identities. This theory resonates with Sonja's experiences, as the fear of exclusion not only affected her social interactions but also her mental health. She often felt like an outsider looking in, yearning for acceptance that felt perpetually out of reach.

Systemic Inequalities   The discrimination Sonja faced was not limited to individual interactions; it was also reflective of systemic inequalities embedded within educational institutions. The lack of LGBTQ representation in school curricula perpetuated a culture of invisibility and misunderstanding. For instance, when discussing historical figures, LGBTQ individuals were often omitted, reinforcing the notion that their contributions were less significant. This systemic oversight not only marginalized Sonja's identity but also contributed to a broader societal narrative that devalued LGBTQ lives. Research by the *Human Rights Campaign* (2018) highlights that inclusive curricula can significantly improve the school climate for LGBTQ students, yet Sonja's early education was devoid of such representation.

Coping Mechanisms   In response to these early experiences of discrimination, Sonja began to develop coping mechanisms that would later inform her activism. She found solace in literature, seeking out stories of LGBTQ individuals who had navigated similar challenges. This not only validated her feelings but also instilled a sense of hope. Additionally, she sought out supportive friendships within the LGBTQ community, which became a crucial lifeline. The importance of peer support in mitigating the effects of discrimination is well-documented; studies show that LGBTQ youth with strong support networks experience lower rates of mental health issues (Ryan et al., 2009).

In conclusion, Sonja Eggerickx's early experiences with discrimination were pivotal in shaping her identity and igniting her passion for activism. These formative moments, characterized by verbal harassment, social exclusion, and systemic inequalities, laid the groundwork for her future endeavors. Through resilience and the support of her community, Sonja transformed her pain into purpose, ultimately becoming a powerful advocate for LGBTQ rights in Belgium. Her journey underscores the critical need for inclusive education and the affirmation of diverse identities in fostering a more equitable society.

Finding support within the LGBTQ community

In the journey of self-discovery and acceptance, finding support within the LGBTQ community is a pivotal experience for many individuals. For Sonja Eggerickx, this support became a sanctuary, a place where shared experiences and understanding fostered a sense of belonging. The LGBTQ community often serves as a crucial lifeline for those grappling with their identities, especially in a society that can be fraught with discrimination and stigma.

The LGBTQ community is characterized by its diversity, encompassing a wide range of identities, experiences, and backgrounds. This diversity is not merely a collection of differences but a rich tapestry that provides emotional and social support to its members. The sense of solidarity within the community allows individuals to connect over shared struggles and triumphs, creating an environment where one can express their true selves without fear of judgment.

The Role of Peer Support

Peer support plays a significant role in the LGBTQ community. It is through peer interactions that individuals can find validation and encouragement. Research indicates that peer support can significantly enhance psychological well-being among LGBTQ youth, helping them navigate the complexities of their identities. According to the *National LGBTQ Task Force*, individuals who engage with supportive peers are more likely to report higher levels of self-esteem and lower levels of depression.

For Sonja, joining local LGBTQ groups marked the beginning of her journey toward self-acceptance. These groups provided her not only with a network of friends but also with mentors who guided her through the challenges of coming out. The importance of mentorship in the LGBTQ community cannot be overstated; mentors often share their own experiences, offering valuable insights and strategies for coping with societal pressures.

Creating Safe Spaces

Safe spaces are essential for fostering a sense of belonging within the LGBTQ community. These environments allow individuals to express themselves freely, engage in discussions about their identities, and seek support without the fear of discrimination. Safe spaces can take many forms, from community centers and support groups to online forums and social media platforms.

Sonja found solace in a local LGBTQ youth center, which not only provided resources but also hosted events that celebrated LGBTQ culture. The center became a hub for activism, education, and social interaction, reinforcing the idea that the community is stronger when individuals come together. The concept of safe spaces aligns with the theory of *intersectionality*, which posits that individuals experience overlapping identities that can compound their experiences of discrimination. By creating inclusive environments, the LGBTQ community acknowledges and addresses these complexities, ensuring that all voices are heard.

Challenges of Finding Support

Despite the advantages of community support, many individuals still face challenges in accessing these resources. In some regions, LGBTQ organizations may be scarce, and individuals may feel isolated due to geographic or social constraints. Additionally, systemic issues such as funding cuts to LGBTQ programs can limit the availability of support services.

Sonja's experience reflects this reality. While she found a supportive network in her local community, she also encountered barriers in accessing resources, particularly in more rural areas of Belgium. This disparity highlights the need for broader advocacy efforts to ensure that LGBTQ individuals in all regions can access the support they need.

The Importance of Representation

Representation within the LGBTQ community is vital for fostering a sense of belonging. When individuals see themselves reflected in leaders, mentors, and media, it reinforces the idea that their identities are valid and worthy of celebration. Representation can also challenge stereotypes and promote a more nuanced understanding of LGBTQ experiences.

Sonja's involvement in LGBTQ activism not only provided her with support but also inspired her to become a role model for others. By sharing her story, she became a source of hope for many young LGBTQ individuals who were struggling with their identities. This cycle of representation and support underscores the importance of visibility in the community.

Conclusion

Finding support within the LGBTQ community is a transformative experience that can profoundly impact an individual's journey toward self-acceptance. Through peer support, safe spaces, and representation, individuals like Sonja Eggerickx can navigate the complexities of their identities while contributing to a larger movement for change. As the LGBTQ community continues to evolve, the importance of fostering inclusive environments remains paramount, ensuring that all members can thrive and support one another in their shared quest for equality and acceptance.

The influence of family and friends

The journey of self-discovery and activism for many individuals within the LGBTQ community is profoundly shaped by the influences of family and friends. For Sonja Eggerickx, these relationships served as both a sanctuary and a catalyst for her burgeoning activism. Understanding this dynamic is crucial, as it reflects not only personal experiences but also broader societal themes surrounding acceptance, identity, and the quest for equality.

Supportive Foundations

From an early age, Sonja was fortunate to have a family that, while initially struggling with the concept of her identity, ultimately became a source of support. Research has shown that familial acceptance can significantly influence the mental health and self-esteem of LGBTQ individuals. According to the *Family Acceptance Project*, youth who perceive familial rejection are at a higher risk for mental health issues, including depression and anxiety, whereas those who feel supported are more likely to thrive.

Sonja's parents, upon learning about her identity, underwent a transformative journey themselves. They attended workshops and engaged with LGBTQ advocacy groups, demonstrating a willingness to learn and grow. This not only helped Sonja feel accepted but also empowered her to embrace her identity fully. The process of acceptance within families can often resemble the stages of grief, as proposed by Elisabeth Kübler-Ross: denial, anger, bargaining, depression, and acceptance. Sonja's family navigated these stages, ultimately arriving at a place of acceptance that fortified her resolve to advocate for LGBTQ rights.

Friendship as a Catalyst

In addition to familial support, Sonja found a vibrant network of friends who shared similar experiences. These friendships were crucial during her coming-out process, providing a sense of belonging that is often pivotal for LGBTQ youth. A study conducted by the *American Psychological Association* highlights that peer support can mitigate feelings of isolation and promote resilience among LGBTQ individuals.

Sonja's friends not only celebrated her identity but also encouraged her to engage in activism. They organized discussions and informal gatherings that provided a safe space for sharing experiences and strategizing on how to address discrimination and advocate for change. This collective effort exemplifies the concept of *social capital*, which refers to the resources available to individuals through their social networks. In Sonja's case, her friends contributed to her social capital, enhancing her confidence and commitment to activism.

Challenges and Conflicts

However, the influence of family and friends was not without its challenges. Sonja encountered moments of conflict, particularly with peers who held more conservative views. These interactions often forced her to confront her beliefs and articulate her identity in a way that was both assertive and educational. The tension between acceptance and rejection within her social circles highlighted the complexities of navigating an LGBTQ identity in a society that can be both supportive and hostile.

Moreover, Sonja's experience reflects the broader societal issues of homophobia and discrimination, which can manifest within familial and friendship dynamics. The *National LGBTQ Task Force* reports that many LGBTQ individuals experience rejection from friends and family, leading to increased vulnerability. Sonja's resilience in the face of such challenges not only strengthened her activism but also inspired those around her to confront their biases and engage in meaningful dialogues about LGBTQ rights.

Conclusion

In summary, the influence of family and friends played a pivotal role in shaping Sonja Eggerickx's journey as an LGBTQ activist. Their support provided a foundation of acceptance that empowered her to embrace her identity and advocate for change. The complexities of these relationships, marked by both support and conflict, underscore the importance of community in the fight for LGBTQ rights. As Sonja navigated her path, she not only transformed her own life but also became a beacon of hope and inspiration for others, illustrating the profound impact that love and acceptance can have in the quest for equality.

Coming out and embracing identity

Overcoming fear and stigma

The journey of embracing one's identity as an LGBTQ individual is often fraught with challenges, particularly the pervasive fear and stigma that society can impose. For many, including Sonja Eggerickx, the process of coming out is not merely a personal revelation; it is a courageous act of defiance against a backdrop of societal prejudices and misconceptions.

Fear, in this context, manifests in various forms—fear of rejection, fear of violence, and fear of being ostracized by family and friends. According to the *American Psychological Association*, this fear can lead to significant psychological distress, including anxiety and depression. The stigma associated with being LGBTQ is rooted in deeply ingrained societal norms and attitudes, which often portray non-heteronormative identities as deviant or abnormal. This stigma can create an internalized sense of shame, leading individuals to suppress their true selves.

To overcome these fears and the associated stigma, individuals often seek support systems. For Sonja, finding a community within the LGBTQ network was pivotal. Research indicates that social support is a critical factor in mitigating the negative effects of stigma. A study by *Meyer (2003)* on minority stress highlights that individuals who have access to supportive networks experience lower levels of psychological distress.

Sonja's experience exemplifies this theory. Surrounded by friends and mentors who embraced her identity, she began to dismantle the internalized fears that had held her back. This process involved several key strategies:

1. **Education**: Understanding the historical and sociopolitical context of LGBTQ identities helped Sonja contextualize her experiences. By learning about the struggles and triumphs of past activists, she found inspiration and validation.

2. **Engagement**: Actively participating in LGBTQ organizations allowed Sonja to confront her fears head-on. By sharing her story and listening to others, she cultivated a sense of belonging and solidarity.

3. **Advocacy**: Transforming her fear into action, Sonja began to advocate for LGBTQ rights. Engaging in activism not only empowered her but also fostered a sense of agency that countered the stigma she faced.

An illustrative example of overcoming stigma can be seen in the *It Gets Better Project*, which was launched in response to a series of tragic suicides among LGBTQ youth. The project aimed to provide hope and support, illustrating that while the journey may be fraught with challenges, there is a community ready to embrace and uplift those who feel marginalized.

Sonja's personal narrative aligns with the findings of *Budge et al.* (2013) that highlight the positive effects of coming out on mental health. The act of coming out, though daunting, can lead to increased self-esteem and a more authentic life. As Sonja navigated her own coming out process, she learned that vulnerability could be a source of strength.

In conclusion, overcoming fear and stigma is a multifaceted process that involves education, community support, and personal advocacy. For Sonja Eggerickx, embracing her identity was not just about self-acceptance; it was about challenging societal norms and paving the way for future generations to live authentically and without fear. The journey is ongoing, but with each step taken, the barriers of fear and stigma begin to crumble, revealing a path toward empowerment and equality.

Discovering personal strength

In the journey of self-acceptance and activism, discovering personal strength is a pivotal moment for many individuals, particularly within the LGBTQ community. For Sonja Eggerickx, this discovery was not merely an internal realization but a transformative process that propelled her into the heart of activism. Understanding this journey involves examining the interplay of identity, resilience, and the socio-cultural environment that shapes an activist's path.

Theoretical Framework

The concept of personal strength can be framed through the lens of psychological resilience. Resilience, as defined by [?], is the process of adapting well in the face of adversity, trauma, tragedy, threats, or significant sources of stress. It encompasses behaviors, thoughts, and actions that can be learned and developed in anyone. For LGBTQ individuals, resilience often manifests as a response to societal discrimination, stigma, and personal challenges related to their sexual orientation or gender identity.

Overcoming Internal Barriers

Sonja's journey began with confronting her own internalized fears and societal expectations. The stigma surrounding LGBTQ identities often leads to feelings of inadequacy and self-doubt. According to [?], the minority stress model suggests that LGBTQ individuals face chronic stress due to their marginalized status, which can hinder self-acceptance. Sonja's initial struggles were characterized by a profound sense of isolation and fear of rejection.

However, through supportive relationships within the LGBTQ community, she began to dismantle these internal barriers. Support systems, as highlighted by [?], play a crucial role in fostering resilience. Sonja found solace in friendships with other activists who shared similar experiences, allowing her to realize that she was not alone. This sense of belonging became a cornerstone of her personal strength.

Embracing Identity

The process of embracing one's identity is often fraught with challenges, but it is also liberating. Sonja's journey involved a conscious decision to accept her sexual orientation and to view it as a source of strength rather than shame. This acceptance can be understood through the theory of self-affirmation, which posits that individuals are motivated to maintain their self-integrity by affirming their self-worth in various domains [?].

By publicly coming out, Sonja not only affirmed her identity but also empowered herself to take action. This act of bravery is echoed in the experiences of many activists who have turned their personal narratives into powerful tools for advocacy. For instance, the act of coming out has been shown to reduce stigma and foster acceptance within communities, as seen in the work of [?].

Finding Strength in Activism

Activism became a vital outlet for Sonja's personal strength. Engaging in activism allowed her to transform her personal struggles into collective action, fostering a sense of purpose and belonging. The act of fighting for LGBTQ rights not only validated her identity but also reinforced her resilience. As noted by [?], collective activism can enhance individual well-being by providing a sense of agency and community.

Sonja's participation in grassroots movements showcased her newfound strength. She organized local events, participated in protests, and collaborated with other activists, amplifying her voice and the voices of those around her. This engagement not only solidified her identity as an activist but also helped her develop critical leadership skills.   For example, during a significant protest in Brussels, Sonja took the stage to speak about her experiences, rallying others to join the cause. This moment was a turning point, as it marked her transition from a hesitant individual to a confident leader.

Conclusion

Discovering personal strength is a multifaceted journey that involves overcoming internal barriers, embracing one's identity, and engaging in activism. For Sonja Eggerickx, this process was instrumental in shaping her into a formidable advocate for LGBTQ rights in Belgium. Her story serves as a testament to the power of resilience and the importance of supportive communities in fostering personal strength. As she continues to inspire others, it becomes clear that the journey of self-discovery is not only vital for individual empowerment but also for the broader movement towards equality and justice.

Embracing LGBTQ activism

Embracing LGBTQ activism was not merely a personal journey for Sonja Eggerickx; it was a profound commitment to fostering a more inclusive and equitable society. This section explores the theoretical foundations of activism, the challenges faced by LGBTQ individuals, and the transformative power of community engagement.

Theoretical Foundations of Activism

Activism can be understood through various theoretical lenses, including social movement theory and intersectionality.   Social movement theory posits that collective action arises from shared grievances and a desire for change. As Sonja discovered her identity, she recognized the systemic inequalities that marginalized LGBTQ individuals.   According to Tilly (2004), collective action is often a response to perceived injustices, which resonated deeply with Sonja's experiences of discrimination during her formative years.

Intersectionality, a term coined by Kimberlé Crenshaw, provides another critical framework for understanding LGBTQ activism.   It emphasizes the interconnectedness of social identities and the unique challenges faced by individuals at the intersection of multiple marginalized identities. Sonja's activism was informed by her understanding that LGBTQ issues could not be divorced from race, gender, and class. This holistic view allowed her to advocate for a more inclusive movement that addressed the needs of all LGBTQ individuals, particularly those from diverse backgrounds.

Challenges in Embracing Activism

Despite her determination, Sonja faced numerous challenges as she embraced her role as an activist. The stigma associated with being LGBTQ remained pervasive in many aspects of society. For instance, she encountered resistance not only from conservative factions but also from individuals within her own community who were hesitant to challenge the status quo. This internal conflict often led to feelings of isolation and self-doubt.

Moreover, the emotional toll of activism cannot be understated. Sonja grappled with the fear of backlash, not only against herself but also against her loved ones. The psychological impact of activism is well-documented; according to a study by McAdam (1986), activists often experience burnout and emotional exhaustion due to the relentless nature of their work. Sonja had to navigate these challenges while maintaining her passion for change.

The Power of Community Engagement

In the face of adversity, Sonja found strength in community engagement. She realized that activism was not a solitary endeavor; it thrived on collaboration and solidarity. By connecting with other LGBTQ individuals and allies, Sonja began to build a support network that provided both emotional and practical resources.

One of the pivotal moments in her journey was her involvement in a local LGBTQ organization. This experience allowed her to witness firsthand the power of grassroots movements. As described by Della Porta and Diani (2006), grassroots activism mobilizes communities to address local issues, creating a sense of ownership and agency among participants. Sonja's commitment to organizing events, workshops, and awareness campaigns exemplified this principle.

For instance, she helped coordinate a series of educational workshops aimed at dismantling stereotypes and fostering understanding among peers. These workshops not only empowered LGBTQ youth but also educated their allies, creating a ripple effect of awareness and acceptance. The impact of such initiatives was profound; participants reported increased confidence in their identities and a greater sense of belonging.

Transformative Moments

Sonja's journey was marked by transformative moments that solidified her commitment to LGBTQ activism. One such moment occurred during a pride march, where she witnessed the overwhelming support from allies and the visibility of LGBTQ individuals. This experience reaffirmed her belief in the importance of representation and visibility in the fight for equality.

Additionally, Sonja's engagement with international LGBTQ organizations broadened her perspective on activism. She participated in conferences that highlighted the global struggle for LGBTQ rights, allowing her to connect with activists from diverse backgrounds. This exposure reinforced the notion that while local challenges may differ, the fight for dignity and respect is universal.

Conclusion

Embracing LGBTQ activism was a transformative journey for Sonja Eggerickx, marked by theoretical insights, personal challenges, and the power of community. Her commitment to activism not only shaped her identity but also laid the groundwork for her future endeavors in advocating for LGBTQ education in Belgium. By understanding the interconnectedness of social identities and mobilizing communities, Sonja emerged as a powerful voice for change, inspiring others to join the fight for equality and justice.

Chapter Two: Fighting for Change

Joining LGBTQ organizations

The beginnings of Sonja's activism

Sonja Eggerickx's journey into activism was not merely a personal awakening; it was a response to the systemic injustices she witnessed throughout her formative years in Belgium. The seeds of her activism were sown in the fertile ground of her childhood experiences, where she first encountered the harsh realities of discrimination and exclusion.

At the tender age of twelve, Sonja faced her first significant challenge when she realized that her identity did not conform to societal norms. The feeling of being different became a weight she carried, compounded by the whispers of prejudice that echoed through the hallways of her school. It was during this time that she began to understand the concept of **intersectionality**, a term coined by Kimberlé Crenshaw in 1989, which highlights how various social identities (such as race, gender, sexuality, and class) intersect to create unique modes of discrimination and privilege. For Sonja, being both a young girl and part of the LGBTQ community meant navigating a complex landscape of bias that often left her feeling isolated.

In her quest for belonging, Sonja sought refuge within the LGBTQ community, where she found not just acceptance but also empowerment. This community became a sanctuary, a space where she could explore her identity without fear of judgment. The support she received was pivotal; it reinforced the idea that activism could be a powerful tool for change. Inspired by the stories of others who had fought against the tide of discrimination, Sonja began to understand her own potential as an activist.

Her early activism was fueled by a series of local workshops and community gatherings that focused on LGBTQ rights. These events often featured speakers who shared their own struggles and triumphs, illustrating the importance of visibility and representation in activism. One particular workshop, titled *"Voices of Change: The Power of Personal Narratives"*, left a lasting impression on Sonja. It emphasized the transformative power of storytelling in activism, a concept rooted in the theory of **narrative identity** proposed by psychologist Dan P. McAdams. This theory posits that individuals create their identities through the stories they tell about themselves, thus shaping their beliefs and actions.

Emboldened by these experiences, Sonja began to engage in grassroots organizing. She volunteered with local LGBTQ organizations, where she learned the intricacies of advocacy and the importance of coalition-building. One of her first significant contributions was helping to organize a pride march in her city, which aimed to raise awareness about LGBTQ issues and promote inclusivity. This event was not without its challenges; Sonja and her fellow organizers faced opposition from conservative groups who sought to undermine their efforts. However, this backlash only fueled Sonja's resolve. She quickly learned the importance of resilience in activism, a lesson echoed in the writings of activist Audre Lorde, who famously stated, "It is not our differences that divide us. It is our inability to recognize, accept, and celebrate those differences."

As she delved deeper into the world of activism, Sonja began to recognize the gaps in LGBTQ education within the Belgian school system. She understood that the lack of inclusive curriculum not only marginalized LGBTQ students but also perpetuated a cycle of ignorance and discrimination among their peers. This realization became a catalyst for her future endeavors, propelling her towards the mission of revolutionizing education for LGBTQ youth.

In summary, the beginnings of Sonja Eggerickx's activism were marked by personal struggles, community support, and a growing awareness of the systemic barriers faced by LGBTQ individuals. Her early experiences laid the groundwork for her future initiatives, igniting a passion for change that would define her life's work. Through the lens of intersectionality and narrative identity, Sonja's journey exemplifies the profound impact of personal experience in shaping an activist's path.

Advocating for LGBTQ rights in Belgium

Belgium has long been recognized as a progressive nation regarding LGBTQ rights, yet the journey to achieve this status was fraught with challenges and resistance. Sonja Eggerickx emerged as a pivotal figure in this landscape, advocating for the rights of LGBTQ individuals and working tirelessly to dismantle the barriers that hindered equality. This section delves into the various dimensions of Sonja's advocacy, highlighting the theoretical frameworks, the problems faced, and the impactful examples that defined her efforts.

Theoretical Frameworks

Advocacy for LGBTQ rights in Belgium can be understood through several theoretical lenses, including social justice theory, intersectionality, and the human rights framework. Social justice theory posits that every individual deserves equal rights and opportunities, which resonates deeply with the LGBTQ movement's core objectives. This theory emphasizes the need for systemic change to address inequalities that marginalized groups face.

Intersectionality, a term coined by Kimberlé Crenshaw, is crucial in understanding how various forms of discrimination can overlap. For LGBTQ individuals, factors such as race, gender, socio-economic status, and disability can compound the challenges they face. Sonja Eggerickx's advocacy was informed by an intersectional approach, recognizing that the fight for LGBTQ rights cannot be isolated from other social justice movements.

The human rights framework further underpins the advocacy efforts by asserting that LGBTQ individuals possess inherent rights that must be respected and protected. This framework provides a legal and moral foundation for Sonja's work, as it aligns with international human rights standards that Belgium is obligated to uphold.

Challenges in Advocacy

Despite Belgium's reputation for progressivism, the road to LGBTQ equality was littered with obstacles. One significant challenge was the persistent societal stigma surrounding LGBTQ identities. Discrimination and prejudice were deeply ingrained in various sectors, including education, healthcare, and employment. Sonja encountered numerous instances where individuals were denied basic rights and services due to their sexual orientation or gender identity.

Moreover, the legal landscape, while improving, still presented hurdles. For instance, although same-sex marriage was legalized in 2003, issues such as adoption rights and access to fertility treatments for same-sex couples remained contentious. This legal ambiguity created a sense of uncertainty within the LGBTQ community, necessitating persistent advocacy to ensure comprehensive rights.

Strategies for Advocacy

Sonja Eggerickx employed a multifaceted approach to advocate for LGBTQ rights in Belgium. One of her primary strategies was community engagement. By organizing workshops, seminars, and community forums, she fostered dialogue between LGBTQ individuals and allies, creating a supportive environment that encouraged the sharing of experiences and resources.

Additionally, Sonja recognized the importance of visibility in advocacy. She utilized media platforms to amplify LGBTQ voices and stories, showcasing the realities faced by the community. Through social media campaigns and collaborations with journalists, she brought attention to issues such as hate crimes, discrimination in the workplace, and mental health challenges, thereby humanizing the statistics often presented in policy discussions.

Impactful Examples

One of Sonja's notable achievements was her involvement in the campaign for the adoption rights of same-sex couples. In 2015, she played a crucial role in a coalition that lobbied the Belgian government to amend existing laws that restricted adoption rights based on sexual orientation. This campaign included public demonstrations, petitions, and direct lobbying of lawmakers. The coalition's efforts culminated in a landmark decision that expanded adoption rights, allowing same-sex couples to adopt children on equal footing with heterosexual couples.

Furthermore, Sonja's advocacy extended to educational institutions, where she worked to implement anti-bullying policies that specifically addressed LGBTQ issues. In collaboration with various schools, she developed training programs for educators, equipping them with the tools to create inclusive environments. This initiative not only raised awareness about LGBTQ rights among students and staff but also contributed to a significant decrease in reported bullying incidents related to sexual orientation.

Conclusion

Sonja Eggerickx's advocacy for LGBTQ rights in Belgium exemplifies the power of grassroots movements in effecting social change. By employing a combination of theoretical frameworks, addressing societal challenges, and implementing strategic initiatives, she has made a lasting impact on the landscape of LGBTQ rights in Belgium. Her work serves as a testament to the ongoing struggle for equality and the importance of continued advocacy in the face of adversity. The journey is far from over, but with leaders like Sonja at the forefront, there is hope for a more inclusive future.

Forming alliances with other activists

In the landscape of activism, the power of collaboration cannot be overstated. For Sonja Eggerickx, forming alliances with other activists was not merely a strategic move; it was a fundamental aspect of her journey towards creating a more inclusive society for LGBTQ individuals in Belgium. The act of uniting diverse voices under a common cause amplifies the impact of advocacy efforts, fosters solidarity, and creates a sense of community among those who share similar goals.

The Importance of Collaboration

Theoretical frameworks such as the *Social Movement Theory* highlight the significance of collective action in achieving social change. According to Tilly (2004), social movements thrive on the mobilization of resources, which includes not only financial support but also human capital and knowledge. By forming alliances, activists can pool their resources, share strategies, and create a more formidable force against systemic oppression.

Sonja understood that LGBTQ rights could not be isolated from other social justice movements. She recognized the intersections of race, gender, and class within the LGBTQ community, which led her to collaborate with activists from various backgrounds. This intersectional approach is supported by Crenshaw's (1989) theory of intersectionality, which argues that individuals experience multiple, overlapping forms of discrimination. By aligning with other marginalized groups, Sonja aimed to address the broader social injustices that affected not just LGBTQ individuals, but also women, people of color, and those with disabilities.

Building Strategic Alliances

Sonja's early involvement with local LGBTQ organizations provided her with a platform to meet like-minded activists. These organizations often hosted workshops, seminars, and community events that emphasized the importance of unity in the fight for rights. One notable example was the annual *Pride Parade*, where various advocacy groups collaborated to raise awareness about LGBTQ issues. Sonja took the initiative to connect with feminist groups, racial justice organizations, and youth advocacy networks, recognizing that a unified front would strengthen their collective message.

A pivotal moment in her activism was the formation of the *Alliance for Equality*, a coalition of various activist groups dedicated to promoting LGBTQ rights in Belgium. This alliance focused on several key areas:

+ **Joint Campaigns:** By launching campaigns that highlighted the interconnectedness of various issues, the alliance was able to reach a broader audience. For instance, they organized a campaign that addressed both LGBTQ rights and racial equality, illustrating how these issues are intertwined.

+ **Shared Resources:** The coalition allowed member organizations to share educational materials, legal resources, and training programs, thereby enhancing the effectiveness of their outreach efforts.

+ **Collective Advocacy:** The alliance provided a platform for activists to collectively advocate for policy changes, making it more challenging for policymakers to ignore their demands.

Challenges in Forming Alliances

Despite the benefits of collaboration, Sonja faced challenges in forming alliances. One significant problem was the existence of differing priorities among various activist groups. For example, while LGBTQ organizations focused primarily on issues such as marriage equality and anti-discrimination laws, feminist groups might prioritize reproductive rights. These differences sometimes led to tensions within the alliance, as activists struggled to balance their unique agendas.

Additionally, the issue of representation within these alliances posed a challenge. Some activists voiced concerns that LGBTQ organizations, particularly those led by white individuals, were not adequately representing the voices of LGBTQ people of color. To address this, Sonja advocated for inclusive practices within the alliance, ensuring that marginalized voices were heard and valued. This commitment to inclusivity not only strengthened the alliance but also enriched the discourse surrounding LGBTQ issues.

Examples of Successful Alliances

Sonja's efforts to form alliances bore fruit in several successful initiatives. One such initiative was the *Safe Schools Project*, which brought together LGBTQ activists, educators, and mental health professionals to develop comprehensive resources for creating safer school environments. This project resulted in the implementation of anti-bullying policies that specifically addressed LGBTQ-related harassment, showcasing the power of collaborative efforts.

Another notable example was the *Pride in Politics* campaign, where LGBTQ activists joined forces with political organizations to advocate for inclusive legislation. This campaign not only raised awareness about LGBTQ issues but also successfully lobbied for the inclusion of LGBTQ history in school curricula, demonstrating how alliances can effectively influence policy.

Conclusion

The formation of alliances with other activists was a cornerstone of Sonja Eggerickx's approach to LGBTQ advocacy. By recognizing the interconnectedness of various social justice movements and actively seeking collaboration, she was able to amplify her impact and create lasting change. The challenges faced in forming these alliances served as valuable lessons, reinforcing the importance of inclusivity and collective action in the ongoing fight for equality. In doing so, Sonja not only contributed to the advancement of LGBTQ rights in Belgium but also laid the groundwork for future generations of activists to continue the work she began.

The power of grassroots movements

Organizing protests and demonstrations

The act of organizing protests and demonstrations serves as a pivotal strategy in the LGBTQ rights movement, particularly for activists like Sonja Eggerickx. These events not only galvanize public support but also raise awareness about pressing issues within the community. The methodology behind effective protest organization can be analyzed through various theoretical frameworks, including social movement theory and collective action theory.

Theoretical Frameworks

Social movement theory posits that collective action arises from shared grievances and a desire for change. According to Tilly (2004), the process of mobilization involves three key components: *recruitment, framing,* and *resource mobilization*. Each component plays a significant role in the success of protests and demonstrations.

$$\text{Mobilization} = \text{Recruitment} + \text{Framing} + \text{Resource Mobilization} \qquad (2)$$

Recruitment refers to the process of engaging individuals and groups to join the cause. Sonja utilized her networks within LGBTQ organizations to recruit volunteers, emphasizing the importance of shared experiences and collective identity.

Framing involves the construction of a narrative that resonates with potential supporters. By articulating the injustices faced by LGBTQ individuals—such as discrimination in schools and workplaces—Sonja framed the protests as not merely events, but as crucial moments for societal change.

Resource mobilization encompasses the strategies employed to secure funding, venues, and materials necessary for organizing protests. Sonja often collaborated with local businesses and community organizations to gather resources, ensuring that protests were well-equipped and effectively publicized.

Challenges in Organizing Protests

Despite the theoretical frameworks supporting protest organization, activists frequently encounter significant challenges. One primary issue is *backlash from conservative groups*, who may oppose LGBTQ rights and mobilize counter-protests. For instance, during a demonstration organized by Sonja in Brussels, counter-protesters attempted to disrupt the event, leading to heightened tensions and confrontations.

Additionally, *logistical challenges* can arise, such as securing permits, coordinating transportation, and ensuring the safety of participants. Sonja's team addressed these challenges by forming alliances with local law enforcement and city officials, fostering a cooperative relationship that facilitated smoother event execution.

Examples of Successful Protests

One notable example of a successful protest organized by Sonja occurred during the annual Pride Month in 2019. With the theme *"Education is a Right, Not a Privilege,"* this demonstration aimed to highlight the need for LGBTQ-inclusive curricula in schools.

The protest drew thousands of participants, showcasing a diverse array of supporters, including students, educators, and parents. Sonja's strategic use of social media platforms to disseminate information and rally support proved effective, as evidenced by the significant turnout.

During the event, participants carried signs emblazoned with slogans such as *"Teach Acceptance, Not Fear"* and *"Every Child Deserves to Learn Their History."* This visual representation of solidarity not only amplified the message but also attracted media attention, furthering the reach of the cause.

The Impact of Protests

The impact of organizing protests extends beyond immediate visibility. Successful demonstrations can lead to tangible changes in policy and public perception. For instance, following the Pride Month protest, Sonja's advocacy efforts culminated in a meeting with key policymakers, resulting in the introduction of a bill aimed at integrating LGBTQ education into the national curriculum.

$$\text{Impact} = \text{Visibility} + \text{Policy Change} + \text{Community Engagement} \qquad (3)$$

In this equation, Visibility refers to the public awareness generated by the protest, Policy Change indicates the legislative outcomes achieved, and Community Engagement reflects the ongoing involvement of community members in advocacy efforts.

In conclusion, organizing protests and demonstrations is a multifaceted endeavor that requires strategic planning, community involvement, and resilience in the face of challenges. Through her efforts, Sonja Eggerickx exemplified how effective protest organization can catalyze change, mobilize support, and foster a sense of unity within the LGBTQ community. The legacy of these actions continues to inspire future generations of activists, underscoring the enduring power of collective action in the pursuit of equality and justice.

Building a community of support

In the pursuit of LGBTQ rights, the establishment of a strong, supportive community is paramount. Sonja Eggerickx understood that activism is not a solitary endeavor; it thrives in the embrace of collective action. A community of support can be defined as a network of individuals and organizations that come together to share resources, knowledge, and emotional backing, fostering resilience and empowerment within the LGBTQ movement.

Theoretical Framework

Theories of social capital, particularly those articulated by Pierre Bourdieu, provide a crucial lens through which to view the importance of community in activism. Bourdieu posits that social capital comprises the networks of relationships among people who live and work in a particular society, enabling them to function effectively. In the context of LGBTQ activism, social capital manifests as the connections that activists forge with one another, which can lead to increased visibility, shared resources, and collective strength.

$$\text{Social Capital} = \text{Networks} + \text{Trust} + \text{Shared Norms} \qquad (4)$$

This equation illustrates that the strength of a community is not merely in numbers but in the quality of relationships and shared values.

Challenges Faced

Despite the theoretical understanding of social capital, building a supportive community is fraught with challenges. One significant problem is the fragmentation within the LGBTQ community itself. Different identities within the spectrum—such as gay, lesbian, bisexual, transgender, and non-binary individuals—often face unique struggles that can lead to divisions rather than unity.

For instance, while gay men may have visibility in media representation, transgender individuals may still grapple with systemic discrimination and lack of recognition. This fragmentation can hinder collective action, as different groups may prioritize divergent issues.

Moreover, external societal pressures—such as homophobia, transphobia, and institutional discrimination—can create an environment of fear and isolation. Activists may find themselves at odds with one another, competing for limited resources, attention, and support.

Strategies for Community Building

To combat these challenges, Sonja focused on several key strategies to build a resilient community of support:

- **Creating Safe Spaces:** Sonja emphasized the need for safe spaces where individuals could express their identities without fear of judgment or backlash. These spaces serve as havens for LGBTQ youth and allies, fostering an environment of acceptance and understanding.

- **Facilitating Open Dialogue:** Encouraging open conversations among diverse groups within the LGBTQ community was crucial. Sonja organized workshops and forums where individuals could share their experiences, challenges, and triumphs, promoting empathy and solidarity.

+ **Resource Sharing and Collaboration:** Sonja recognized that pooling resources was vital for the community's sustainability. By collaborating with local organizations, activists could share educational materials, training programs, and funding opportunities, enhancing the overall capacity for advocacy.

+ **Mentorship Programs:** Establishing mentorship initiatives allowed seasoned activists to guide newcomers, fostering a sense of belonging and continuity within the movement. These programs not only empower individuals but also create a legacy of knowledge and experience that strengthens the community.

Examples of Success

One notable example of community building in action was the annual Pride festival organized by Sonja and her allies. This event not only celebrated LGBTQ identities but also served as a platform for various organizations to showcase their work and connect with potential supporters. The festival attracted thousands of attendees, fostering a sense of unity and shared purpose.

Additionally, Sonja's collaboration with schools to implement LGBTQ-inclusive curricula provided a tangible way to build community support among educators, students, and families. By engaging with educational institutions, Sonja created a network of allies who were committed to fostering inclusive environments for LGBTQ youth.

Conclusion

In conclusion, building a community of support is a foundational aspect of effective LGBTQ activism. Through the lens of social capital theory, it becomes evident that the strength of a movement lies in its ability to forge meaningful connections among its members. While challenges such as fragmentation and societal pressures persist, strategies like creating safe spaces, facilitating dialogue, sharing resources, and establishing mentorship programs can empower individuals and unite the community. Sonja Eggerickx's efforts exemplify the transformative power of community in the ongoing fight for LGBTQ rights in Belgium and beyond.

Gaining recognition for LGBTQ issues

The journey toward gaining recognition for LGBTQ issues in Belgium has been a multifaceted endeavor, characterized by both grassroots activism and strategic outreach. At the heart of this movement lies the understanding that visibility is a precursor to acceptance. Sonja Eggerickx recognized early on that, in order to effect change, the stories, struggles, and triumphs of LGBTQ individuals needed to be brought to the forefront of public consciousness.

Theoretical Framework

In exploring the recognition of LGBTQ issues, we can draw upon the Social Movement Theory, which posits that social movements arise when groups of people mobilize to address grievances and pursue collective goals. The theory emphasizes the importance of identity, collective action, and political opportunity structures. In the case of LGBTQ activism, the recognition of issues is not merely about visibility; it is also about creating a narrative that resonates with the broader public, thereby leveraging political opportunities to advocate for change.

$$\text{Recognition} = f(\text{Visibility}, \text{Narrative}, \text{Political Opportunity}) \qquad (5)$$

Where f represents a function that determines recognition based on the interplay of visibility, narrative construction, and the existing political landscape.

Challenges Faced

Despite the progress made, gaining recognition for LGBTQ issues has not been without its challenges. One of the most significant barriers has been societal stigma, which has historically marginalized LGBTQ voices. This stigma is often perpetuated by a lack of understanding and misinformation about LGBTQ identities and experiences. For instance, during the early years of Sonja's activism, many educational institutions were resistant to addressing LGBTQ topics, fearing backlash from conservative groups and parents.

Moreover, institutional inertia within educational systems posed another challenge. Many educators were either unaware of the need for LGBTQ-inclusive curricula or lacked the resources to implement such changes. This created a dissonance between the advocacy efforts of activists like Sonja and the realities faced by schools.

Strategies for Recognition

To combat these challenges, Sonja employed a variety of strategies aimed at gaining recognition for LGBTQ issues. One of the most effective was the use of personal storytelling as a tool for advocacy. By sharing her own experiences and those of others within the community, she was able to humanize the issues at stake. This approach not only fostered empathy but also encouraged dialogue around LGBTQ topics in spaces where silence had previously prevailed.

> *"When we share our stories, we connect on a human level. It's hard to ignore the pain and joy of someone's lived experience."*

Additionally, Sonja understood the importance of allyship in amplifying LGBTQ voices. By forming alliances with other social justice movements, she was able to broaden the reach of LGBTQ issues. Collaborations with feminist groups, racial justice organizations, and youth advocacy networks helped to create a unified front that was difficult for policymakers to overlook.

Examples of Recognition

One notable example of gaining recognition for LGBTQ issues in Belgium was the campaign for the inclusion of LGBTQ topics in the national education curriculum. Through persistent advocacy, Sonja and her colleagues were able to engage with policymakers, educators, and the public to highlight the need for an inclusive curriculum that addressed the realities of LGBTQ youth.

In 2018, the Belgian government announced a commitment to integrating LGBTQ education into schools, a significant victory for activists. This decision was influenced by a series of high-profile reports and studies that demonstrated the positive impact of inclusive education on student well-being and academic performance.

$$\text{Impact of Inclusive Education} = \frac{\text{Reduction in Bullying}}{\text{Increase in Student Well-being}} \quad (6)$$

This equation illustrates the positive correlation between inclusive education and a decrease in bullying incidents, as well as an increase in overall student well-being.

Media Engagement

Another critical avenue for recognition was media engagement. Sonja recognized that traditional media outlets could serve as powerful platforms for advocacy. By participating in interviews, writing op-eds, and utilizing social media, she was able to bring LGBTQ issues into the public discourse. The portrayal of LGBTQ individuals in the media has a profound impact on societal perceptions, and Sonja worked diligently to ensure that these portrayals were both accurate and positive.

The rise of social media also played a pivotal role in this recognition process. Platforms like Twitter, Instagram, and Facebook allowed for the rapid dissemination of information and the mobilization of support. Hashtags such as #LGBTQEducation and #InclusiveSchools became rallying cries for activists, facilitating a global conversation about the importance of LGBTQ inclusion in education.

Conclusion

In summary, gaining recognition for LGBTQ issues in Belgium was not an isolated effort but rather a concerted movement that involved multiple strategies and collaborative efforts. Through personal storytelling, strategic alliances, media engagement, and persistent advocacy, Sonja Eggerickx and her fellow activists were able to elevate LGBTQ issues to a place of visibility and significance within the public sphere. As a result, they not only transformed the educational landscape in Belgium but also laid the groundwork for future generations of activists to continue the fight for equality and recognition.

Chapter Three: Revolutionizing Education

Recognizing the need for LGBTQ education

The lack of LGBTQ-inclusive curriculum

The absence of LGBTQ-inclusive curriculum in educational institutions has been a significant barrier to achieving equality and acceptance for LGBTQ individuals. This gap in education not only perpetuates ignorance but also fosters an environment where prejudice can thrive. As Sonja Eggerickx recognized early in her activism, the educational system plays a crucial role in shaping societal attitudes towards LGBTQ individuals.

Theoretical Framework

Theoretical frameworks surrounding education and inclusivity suggest that curricula must reflect the diversity of society to promote understanding and acceptance among students. According to critical pedagogy, as posited by Paulo Freire, education should empower marginalized voices and challenge oppressive structures. Without LGBTQ representation in the curriculum, students are deprived of the opportunity to learn about the rich history and contributions of LGBTQ individuals, leading to a narrow understanding of human experiences.

Problems Arising from Lack of Inclusion

The consequences of not including LGBTQ perspectives in educational curricula are profound. Firstly, students who identify as LGBTQ often feel alienated and invisible in a learning environment that fails to acknowledge their existence. This invisibility can lead to increased rates of depression, anxiety, and suicidal ideation among LGBTQ youth. The *Trevor Project* reported that LGBTQ youth who learn about LGBTQ issues in school are 23% less likely to report a suicide attempt than those who do not.

Moreover, the lack of LGBTQ-inclusive curriculum contributes to the perpetuation of stereotypes and misinformation. For instance, without education on the history of LGBTQ rights movements, students may grow up with misconceptions about LGBTQ identities, leading to discrimination and bullying. The *National School Climate Survey* conducted by GLSEN found that 60% of LGBTQ students felt unsafe in school due to their sexual orientation, with 40% experiencing harassment.

Examples of Exclusion

In Belgium, as in many countries, the educational curriculum has traditionally focused on a heteronormative perspective, often ignoring LGBTQ contributions to society. For instance, historical figures such as Marsha P. Johnson and Harvey Milk are rarely mentioned in history classes, leaving students unaware of the struggles and triumphs that have shaped the LGBTQ rights movement.

Furthermore, the lack of inclusive materials, such as textbooks that feature LGBTQ characters or stories, further alienates LGBTQ students. A survey conducted by the *Human Rights Campaign* found that 70% of LGBTQ youth reported that their school did not provide any LGBTQ-inclusive materials, leading to a significant knowledge gap among students regarding LGBTQ issues.

The Need for Change

To address the lack of LGBTQ-inclusive curriculum, educational institutions must take proactive steps to implement comprehensive LGBTQ education. This includes revising existing curricula to incorporate LGBTQ history, literature, and social issues, as well as training educators on LGBTQ inclusivity. By fostering an inclusive environment, schools can create safe spaces for all students, regardless of their sexual orientation or gender identity.

In conclusion, the lack of LGBTQ-inclusive curriculum is a pressing issue that requires immediate attention. As Sonja Eggerickx's activism demonstrated, education is a powerful tool for change. By advocating for an inclusive curriculum, we can empower future generations to embrace diversity and combat discrimination, ultimately contributing to a more equitable society for all.

The impact on LGBTQ youth

The impact of a lack of LGBTQ-inclusive education on youth is profound and multifaceted. Research consistently shows that LGBTQ youth face unique challenges that can significantly affect their mental, emotional, and social well-being. The absence of representation and support within educational settings often leads to feelings of isolation, anxiety, and depression among these young individuals.

One of the primary issues is the prevalence of bullying and harassment in schools. According to the 2019 National School Climate Survey conducted by the Gay, Lesbian and Straight Education Network (GLSEN), approximately 70.1% of LGBTQ students reported being bullied in school because of their sexual orientation, and 59.1% reported being bullied because of their gender identity. This kind of victimization can lead to severe consequences, including a heightened risk of mental health issues such as depression and suicidal ideation.

$$\text{Mental Health Impact} = f(\text{Bullying, Isolation, Lack of Support}) \quad (7)$$

Where: - f represents the function determining mental health outcomes, - Bullying is quantified by the frequency and severity of incidents, - Isolation refers to the lack of peer support and community, - Lack of Support encompasses the absence of affirming adults and resources.

Moreover, the lack of inclusive curriculum contributes to feelings of invisibility among LGBTQ youth. When students do not see themselves represented in the material they study, it can reinforce the notion that their identities are not valid or worthy of acknowledgment. This lack of representation can diminish their self-esteem and hinder their personal development. A study by the Human Rights Campaign (HRC) found that LGBTQ youth who attend schools with inclusive curricula report feeling safer and more supported than those who do not.

In addition, the absence of LGBTQ-inclusive education can lead to a lack of understanding among non-LGBTQ peers. This ignorance can perpetuate stereotypes and foster an environment of discrimination. For instance, when heterosexual students are not educated about LGBTQ issues, they may inadvertently contribute to a culture of intolerance. This highlights the importance of comprehensive educational programs that not only support LGBTQ students but also educate the entire student body.

$$\text{Peer Understanding} = \text{Education} \times \text{Inclusion} \quad (8)$$

Where: - Peer Understanding is the level of empathy and support from non-LGBTQ peers, - Education refers to the quality and extent of LGBTQ-related content in the curriculum, - Inclusion signifies the active participation of LGBTQ individuals in school activities and discussions.

The emotional toll of navigating these challenges can be significant. LGBTQ youth are at a higher risk for mental health issues compared to their heterosexual counterparts. According to the Trevor Project's National Survey on LGBTQ Youth Mental Health 2021, 42% of LGBTQ youth seriously considered attempting suicide in the past year, and 94% of LGBTQ youth reported experiencing symptoms of anxiety. These alarming statistics underscore the urgent need for educational reform that prioritizes LGBTQ inclusivity.

Furthermore, the lack of support from educators can exacerbate these issues. When teachers and school staff are not trained to address LGBTQ issues or are indifferent to the needs of LGBTQ students, it creates an unwelcoming environment. This lack of support can lead to disengagement from school and lower academic performance. A study published in the Journal of Educational Psychology found that LGBTQ students who felt supported by their teachers had higher academic achievement and lower levels of absenteeism.

$$\text{Academic Performance} = \text{Support} + \text{Inclusion} - \text{Discrimination} \qquad (9)$$

Where: - Academic Performance is measured by grades, attendance, and engagement, - Support includes teacher and peer support, - Inclusion reflects the representation of LGBTQ issues in the curriculum, - Discrimination accounts for negative experiences related to identity.

In conclusion, the impact of a lack of LGBTQ-inclusive education on youth is profound, affecting their mental health, sense of belonging, and academic success. By recognizing and addressing these issues, educators and policymakers can create a more inclusive environment that empowers LGBTQ youth to thrive. The work of activists like Sonja Eggerickx is crucial in advocating for these necessary changes, ensuring that all students can learn in a safe and supportive environment that acknowledges and celebrates their identities.

Sonja's mission to change the system

Sonja Eggerickx recognized early on that the lack of LGBTQ-inclusive curriculum in Belgium's educational system posed a significant barrier to the acceptance and understanding of LGBTQ identities among students. This gap not only perpetuated ignorance but also contributed to an environment where discrimination thrived. The absence of representation in educational materials meant that LGBTQ youth often felt invisible, leading to a myriad of psychological and social issues, including increased rates of depression and anxiety.

In her pursuit to change the system, Sonja drew upon critical theories of education, particularly those that emphasize the importance of inclusivity and representation. The concept of *culturally responsive pedagogy* was central to her mission, which posits that education should reflect the diverse backgrounds of all students. According to Ladson-Billings (1994), culturally relevant teaching empowers students by validating their identities and experiences. Sonja aimed to implement this framework within the Belgian educational landscape, advocating for a curriculum that not only included LGBTQ history and contributions but also addressed the specific challenges faced by LGBTQ students.

One of the primary problems Sonja encountered was the resistance from traditional educational institutions that were hesitant to embrace change. Many educators and policymakers viewed LGBTQ education as a controversial topic, fearing backlash from parents and conservative groups. This resistance was compounded by societal stigma surrounding LGBTQ issues, which often led to a reluctance to engage in conversations about sexual orientation and gender identity within the classroom.

To combat these challenges, Sonja employed a multifaceted approach. She organized workshops and training sessions for educators to equip them with the necessary tools and knowledge to create inclusive classrooms. By fostering an understanding of LGBTQ issues among educators, she sought to dismantle preconceived notions and biases that often hindered progress. For instance, during a workshop at a local teachers' conference, Sonja presented data illustrating the positive impact of inclusive education on student well-being, including a *decrease in bullying incidents* and an *increase in academic performance* among LGBTQ students.

Furthermore, Sonja leveraged the power of storytelling as a means of advocacy. She encouraged LGBTQ individuals to share their experiences, thereby humanizing the issues at hand and fostering empathy among educators and students alike. By highlighting personal narratives, Sonja aimed to create a sense of urgency and importance around the need for systemic change. She often cited the work of scholars like hooks (1994), who emphasized the transformative potential of narrative in education, arguing that stories can bridge gaps in understanding and inspire action.

In addition to grassroots efforts, Sonja recognized the importance of policy change in achieving her mission. She began to engage with local and national policymakers, advocating for the integration of LGBTQ topics into the national curriculum. Her efforts culminated in the drafting of a proposal for the *LGBTQ*

Education Act, which aimed to mandate the inclusion of LGBTQ history and issues in schools across Belgium. This legislative push was met with both support and opposition, highlighting the ongoing societal divide regarding LGBTQ rights.

Despite the challenges, Sonja's unwavering commitment to changing the system began to yield results. In 2018, after years of advocacy, a pilot program was launched in several schools across Belgium, introducing LGBTQ-inclusive materials and training for educators. The program was met with enthusiasm from students and educators alike, showcasing the potential for a more inclusive educational environment. Early feedback indicated a marked improvement in student engagement and a reduction in instances of bullying, reinforcing the need for continued efforts in this direction.

Sonja's mission to change the system was not just about implementing a curriculum; it was about fostering a culture of acceptance and understanding within schools. By addressing the systemic barriers that marginalized LGBTQ identities, she aimed to create an educational landscape where all students could thrive, free from discrimination and prejudice. Her work laid the groundwork for a more inclusive future, inspiring educators, students, and activists to join the fight for equality.

In summary, Sonja Eggerickx's mission to change the system encompassed a comprehensive approach that included advocacy, education, and policy reform. Through her dedication and resilience, she not only sought to transform the educational experience for LGBTQ students but also aimed to shift societal perceptions, paving the way for a more inclusive and equitable society.

Founding the LGBTQ Education Foundation

Creating safe spaces for LGBTQ students

Creating safe spaces for LGBTQ students is not merely an act of kindness; it is a fundamental necessity for fostering an inclusive educational environment where all students can thrive. The concept of a safe space is rooted in the idea that individuals, particularly those from marginalized communities, should have a refuge where they can express their identities without fear of discrimination, harassment, or violence. This section explores the theoretical underpinnings, challenges, and practical examples of establishing such environments.

Theoretical Framework

The need for safe spaces can be understood through various theoretical lenses, including *Critical Pedagogy* and *Queer Theory*. Critical Pedagogy, as articulated by Paulo Freire, emphasizes the importance of dialogue and the empowerment of marginalized voices. It posits that education should be a collaborative process that challenges oppressive structures. In the context of LGBTQ students, creating a safe space aligns with Freire's ideals by providing a platform for these students to share their experiences, thus validating their identities and fostering a sense of belonging.

Queer Theory further complements this framework by questioning normative assumptions about gender and sexuality. It advocates for the deconstruction of binary classifications and encourages the recognition of diverse identities. By applying these theories, educators can create environments that not only acknowledge but celebrate the multiplicity of LGBTQ identities.

Challenges to Creating Safe Spaces

Despite the theoretical support for safe spaces, numerous challenges persist. One significant barrier is the pervasive stigma surrounding LGBTQ identities. According to the *National School Climate Survey* (2019), nearly 60% of LGBTQ students reported feeling unsafe at school due to their sexual orientation. This statistic underscores the urgent need for intervention.

Moreover, institutional resistance can hinder the establishment of safe spaces. Many educational institutions may lack the resources or political will to implement inclusive policies. As highlighted by the *Human Rights Campaign* (2020), schools often face pushback from parents or community members who oppose LGBTQ-inclusive curricula or policies. This resistance can lead to a hostile environment for both students and educators advocating for change.

Practical Examples

Creating safe spaces requires intentionality and collaboration. One exemplary model is the establishment of *GSA (Gender and Sexuality Alliance)* clubs in schools. These student-led organizations provide a forum for LGBTQ students and their allies to come together, share experiences, and advocate for their rights. Research by *The Trevor Project* (2021) indicates that students who participate in GSAs report lower levels of bullying and higher levels of self-esteem.

Another effective strategy is the implementation of comprehensive training programs for educators. For instance, the *Safe Zone* training initiative equips teachers with the knowledge and skills to support LGBTQ students effectively.

This program not only educates staff about LGBTQ issues but also fosters a culture of inclusivity within the school. A study by *GLSEN* (2020) found that schools with trained faculty members reported a more positive school climate for LGBTQ students.

Finally, creating physical safe spaces within schools, such as LGBTQ resource centers or designated safe rooms, can provide students with a sanctuary where they can seek support and guidance. These spaces should be visible and accessible, signaling to students that their identities are valued and respected.

Conclusion

In conclusion, creating safe spaces for LGBTQ students is an essential component of fostering an inclusive educational environment. By grounding these efforts in critical pedagogical and queer theoretical frameworks, addressing the challenges faced, and implementing practical strategies, educators can significantly impact the lives of LGBTQ students. As Sonja Eggerickx's activism demonstrates, the creation of such spaces is not merely a goal; it is a moral imperative that can lead to transformative change within educational institutions and society at large.

Developing comprehensive educational resources

In the quest for LGBTQ-inclusive education, the development of comprehensive educational resources is paramount. These resources serve as the backbone of educational reform, providing educators with the tools necessary to foster an inclusive learning environment. This section explores the theoretical foundations, challenges faced, and practical examples of effective educational resources designed to support LGBTQ students.

Theoretical Foundations

The development of educational resources for LGBTQ inclusion is grounded in several key theories. One such theory is the **Social Constructivist Theory**, which posits that knowledge is constructed through social interactions and experiences. This theory emphasizes the importance of context in learning, suggesting that educational materials must reflect diverse identities and experiences to be effective. According to Vygotsky's principles, learning occurs within a social context, and resources that incorporate LGBTQ narratives can enhance understanding and acceptance among students.

Moreover, the **Critical Pedagogy** framework, as articulated by Paulo Freire, advocates for an education that empowers marginalized voices. Freire's approach encourages educators to critically engage with the content and question societal norms, making it essential for educational resources to challenge heteronormative assumptions and promote inclusivity.

Challenges in Resource Development

Despite the theoretical support for comprehensive educational resources, several challenges persist. One significant obstacle is the **lack of funding** allocated for the development of LGBTQ-inclusive materials. Many educational institutions prioritize traditional curricula, leaving little room for the incorporation of diverse perspectives. This financial constraint limits the ability to produce high-quality resources that reflect the needs of LGBTQ students.

Another challenge is the **resistance from stakeholders**, including parents, educators, and policymakers. Some individuals may perceive LGBTQ-inclusive resources as controversial or unnecessary, leading to pushback against their implementation. This resistance can hinder the adoption of comprehensive materials, perpetuating a cycle of exclusion and misunderstanding.

Furthermore, the **variability in educational standards** across regions complicates the development of universal resources. Different educational systems may have distinct requirements and cultural contexts, necessitating a tailored approach to resource creation. This variability can result in inconsistencies in the availability and quality of LGBTQ educational materials.

Examples of Effective Educational Resources

To address these challenges, various organizations and educators have developed innovative resources that promote LGBTQ inclusivity. One notable example is the **LGBTQ Inclusive Curriculum Toolkit**, created by the Human Rights Campaign. This toolkit provides educators with lesson plans, discussion guides, and assessment tools designed to integrate LGBTQ topics into existing curricula. By offering practical strategies and resources, the toolkit empowers teachers to create inclusive classrooms while addressing potential resistance from stakeholders.

Another exemplary initiative is the **Safe Schools Coalition**, which has developed a range of resources aimed at fostering safe and inclusive environments for LGBTQ students. Their materials include training modules for educators, student handbooks, and anti-bullying policies that specifically address LGBTQ issues. These resources not only promote awareness but also provide actionable steps for creating supportive school climates.

Additionally, the **Gender Spectrum** organization has produced a comprehensive guide titled *Creating Gender Inclusive Schools*. This resource offers insights into understanding gender diversity, practical strategies for supporting transgender and non-binary students, and recommendations for policy changes. By focusing on gender inclusivity, this guide exemplifies how educational resources can address specific aspects of LGBTQ identity while promoting a broader understanding of diversity.

Conclusion

The development of comprehensive educational resources is a critical component of LGBTQ activism in education. Grounded in theoretical frameworks such as Social Constructivism and Critical Pedagogy, these resources aim to create inclusive learning environments that empower LGBTQ students. Despite facing challenges such as funding limitations and resistance from stakeholders, innovative examples like the LGBTQ Inclusive Curriculum Toolkit and the Safe Schools Coalition demonstrate the potential for positive change. As educational institutions continue to prioritize inclusivity, the ongoing development of comprehensive resources will play a vital role in shaping a more equitable future for all students.

$$\text{Inclusivity} = \frac{\text{Diversity} + \text{Access}}{\text{Resistance}} \tag{10}$$

Collaborating with schools and educators

In the pursuit of creating a more inclusive educational environment for LGBTQ students, collaboration with schools and educators emerges as a pivotal strategy. This collaboration is not merely a procedural formality; it represents a profound commitment to transforming educational spaces into safe havens that affirm and celebrate diversity. The foundation of this collaborative effort rests on several theoretical frameworks, including social constructivism, which emphasizes the importance of social interactions in learning, and critical pedagogy, which advocates for an education that is both liberating and empowering.

Theoretical Frameworks

Social constructivism posits that knowledge is constructed through social interactions and experiences. In the context of LGBTQ education, this means that when educators actively engage with LGBTQ issues, they contribute to a richer understanding of diversity among all students. According to Vygotsky's theory of social development, learning occurs in a social context, suggesting that educators play a crucial role in shaping students' perceptions of identity and acceptance. This approach encourages collaborative learning environments where students can explore and discuss LGBTQ topics openly, fostering empathy and understanding.

Critical pedagogy, on the other hand, challenges traditional power dynamics in education. It advocates for a curriculum that reflects the experiences and histories of marginalized groups, including LGBTQ individuals. By integrating LGBTQ narratives into the curriculum, educators can dismantle oppressive structures and promote a more equitable educational landscape. Freire's concept of dialogue is particularly relevant here; it underscores the importance of conversation and reflection in the learning process. Through dialogue, educators and students can confront biases and misconceptions, paving the way for a more inclusive educational experience.

Identifying Problems

However, the path to collaboration is fraught with challenges. One significant problem is the lack of training and resources for educators regarding LGBTQ issues. Many teachers may feel ill-equipped to address these topics due to their own biases or a lack of understanding. This gap in knowledge can perpetuate a culture of silence around LGBTQ identities, leaving students feeling isolated and unsupported.

Furthermore, institutional resistance can pose a significant barrier. Some schools may have policies that inadvertently marginalize LGBTQ students, such as dress codes that do not accommodate gender expression or curricula that exclude LGBTQ history. These policies can create an environment where LGBTQ students do not feel safe or valued, ultimately hindering their academic success and emotional well-being.

Strategies for Collaboration

To address these challenges, effective strategies for collaboration must be employed. First and foremost, professional development programs focused on LGBTQ education should be implemented. These programs can provide educators with the knowledge and skills necessary to create inclusive classrooms. Workshops can cover topics such as understanding gender identity, recognizing the impact of bullying, and implementing LGBTQ-inclusive curricula.

For example, the LGBTQ Education Foundation can partner with local school districts to facilitate training sessions that empower educators to address LGBTQ issues confidently. These sessions could include guest speakers from the LGBTQ community, interactive discussions, and practical strategies for integrating LGBTQ topics into existing curricula.

In addition to professional development, fostering strong relationships with LGBTQ advocacy organizations can enhance collaboration. Schools can invite representatives from these organizations to participate in school events, such as Pride Month celebrations or diversity fairs. By involving the community, schools can create a more supportive atmosphere for LGBTQ students and educate the broader student body about LGBTQ issues.

Case Studies

Several successful case studies exemplify effective collaboration between LGBTQ organizations and educational institutions. One notable example is the partnership between the LGBTQ Education Foundation and a network of schools in Belgium. This initiative involved the development of an LGBTQ-inclusive curriculum that was piloted in several schools. Feedback from both educators and students indicated a significant increase in awareness and acceptance of LGBTQ identities, as well as a decrease in incidents of bullying.

Another case study involves a school district in the United States that implemented a comprehensive LGBTQ training program for its educators. The program included workshops on inclusive teaching practices, the importance of representation in the curriculum, and strategies for supporting LGBTQ students. As a result, the district reported a marked improvement in the school climate, with students feeling safer and more supported.

Conclusion

In conclusion, collaborating with schools and educators is a vital component of advancing LGBTQ education. By leveraging theoretical frameworks such as social constructivism and critical pedagogy, stakeholders can create meaningful change in educational environments. Despite the challenges that may arise, strategic partnerships, professional development, and community involvement can lead to the successful implementation of LGBTQ-inclusive practices. Ultimately, these efforts contribute to a more equitable educational landscape where all students, regardless of their sexual orientation or gender identity, can thrive.

Chapter Four: Breaking Down Barriers

Overcoming resistance and backlash

Facing societal and institutional challenges

The journey of LGBTQ activists like Sonja Eggerickx is fraught with societal and institutional challenges that often serve as formidable barriers to progress. These challenges manifest in various forms, ranging from overt discrimination to subtle biases embedded within the fabric of societal norms and institutional policies. Understanding these obstacles is crucial to appreciating the resilience and determination required to advocate for change.

Societal Challenges

Societal challenges encompass the attitudes, beliefs, and behaviors of individuals and communities that perpetuate discrimination against LGBTQ individuals. In many cultures, traditional gender roles and heteronormative standards dominate, creating an environment where deviations from the norm are met with resistance or hostility. This societal backdrop can lead to widespread stigma and marginalization of LGBTQ individuals, complicating efforts to promote acceptance and equality.

Examples of Societal Resistance   One poignant example of societal resistance can be observed in the backlash against LGBTQ rights movements, particularly during pivotal moments such as Pride marches or legislative initiatives aimed at expanding rights. Activists often face protests from conservative groups that advocate for the preservation of traditional values, portraying LGBTQ rights as a threat to societal stability. This opposition can manifest in public demonstrations, negative media portrayals, and even legislative efforts to roll back existing rights.

Moreover, societal attitudes can significantly influence the experiences of LGBTQ youth. Research indicates that LGBTQ youth are at a higher risk of experiencing bullying, harassment, and mental health issues compared to their heterosexual peers. This phenomenon is exacerbated by the lack of supportive environments in schools, where educators may be ill-equipped to address LGBTQ issues or may hold their own biases.

Institutional Challenges

Institutional challenges refer to the policies, practices, and structures within organizations—be it educational institutions, government bodies, or corporate entities—that can hinder the advancement of LGBTQ rights. These challenges often stem from a lack of representation and understanding of LGBTQ issues among decision-makers, leading to policies that fail to address the unique needs of LGBTQ individuals.

Examples of Institutional Barriers   For instance, in the educational system, the absence of an LGBTQ-inclusive curriculum perpetuates ignorance and reinforces stereotypes.   Many schools lack comprehensive policies to protect LGBTQ students from discrimination and bullying, resulting in unsafe learning environments. Sonja Eggerickx's advocacy for LGBTQ education highlights the critical need for institutional change, as she sought to implement policies that promote inclusivity and support for LGBTQ students.

Additionally, institutional resistance can be observed in legislative bodies where LGBTQ rights are debated. Lawmakers may face pressure from constituents who oppose LGBTQ rights, leading to watered-down legislation or outright rejection of proposed bills. This dynamic illustrates the interplay between societal attitudes and institutional decision-making, as elected officials often reflect the views of their constituents rather than championing progressive policies.

The Intersection of Societal and Institutional Challenges

The challenges faced by LGBTQ activists are not isolated; rather, they intersect and compound one another. Societal attitudes can influence institutional policies, while institutional failures can reinforce negative societal perceptions. This cyclical relationship creates a daunting landscape for activists like Sonja Eggerickx, who must navigate both realms to effect meaningful change.

To combat these challenges, activists employ various strategies, including grassroots organizing, public awareness campaigns, and coalition-building with allies across different sectors. By fostering dialogue and education, they aim to shift societal perceptions and advocate for institutional reforms that promote equality and inclusivity.

In conclusion, the societal and institutional challenges faced by LGBTQ activists are complex and multifaceted. Understanding these obstacles is essential to appreciating the courage and determination of individuals like Sonja Eggerickx, who tirelessly work to dismantle barriers and create a more equitable society for all. As the fight for LGBTQ rights continues, it is imperative to address these challenges head-on, fostering a culture of acceptance and understanding that transcends societal and institutional boundaries.

Confronting prejudice and discrimination

Confronting prejudice and discrimination is a central challenge for any activist, and for Sonja Eggerickx, it was a reality she faced head-on throughout her career. Prejudice, defined as an unjustified or incorrect attitude towards an individual based solely on their membership in a social group, manifests in various forms, including homophobia, transphobia, and systemic discrimination. Discrimination, on the other hand, refers to the actions taken based on these prejudiced beliefs, often resulting in exclusion or marginalization of LGBTQ individuals in various aspects of life, including education, employment, and healthcare.

Theoretical Framework

To understand the dynamics of prejudice and discrimination, we can draw upon social identity theory, which posits that individuals derive part of their identity from the groups to which they belong. This framework suggests that when individuals identify strongly with a particular group, they may develop an in-group bias, leading to negative attitudes towards out-groups. For LGBTQ individuals, this often translates into a dual struggle: navigating their identity while confronting societal norms that favor heteronormativity.

$$\text{Prejudice} = f(\text{Social Identity, Cultural Norms})$$

Where f represents the function of how social identity and cultural norms interact to produce prejudiced attitudes.

Challenges Faced by Sonja

Sonja encountered numerous challenges as she confronted prejudice and discrimination in her activism. One significant instance occurred during her early involvement with LGBTQ organizations in Belgium, where she faced hostility not only from conservative groups but also from individuals within more liberal circles who were reluctant to address LGBTQ issues openly. This reluctance often stemmed from a fear of backlash or social ostracism.

For example, during a community meeting aimed at discussing the implementation of LGBTQ-inclusive policies in local schools, Sonja faced a barrage of criticisms from parents who argued that such policies would corrupt the youth. This situation exemplified the pervasive prejudice that activists like Sonja had to navigate.

Strategies for Confrontation

To effectively confront these attitudes, Sonja employed several strategies:

1. **Education and Awareness**: Sonja recognized that many prejudiced views stemmed from misinformation and lack of understanding. She initiated workshops and seminars that educated both parents and educators about LGBTQ issues, emphasizing the importance of inclusivity and the detrimental effects of discrimination on youth mental health.

2. **Personal Storytelling**: By sharing her own experiences as a member of the LGBTQ community, Sonja humanized the issues at hand. Personal narratives often resonate more deeply with individuals than statistics or abstract concepts. This approach was particularly effective in bridging gaps between differing viewpoints.

3. **Coalition Building**: Sonja understood the power of alliances. By forming coalitions with other marginalized groups, she was able to amplify her voice and challenge discrimination on multiple fronts. For instance, partnering with feminist organizations helped to address the intersectionality of gender and sexual orientation, fostering a more comprehensive approach to activism.

4. **Advocacy and Lobbying**: Sonja also engaged in direct advocacy, lobbying for policy changes that would protect LGBTQ rights. This included drafting proposals for inclusive educational policies and meeting with lawmakers to discuss the necessity of legal protections against discrimination.

The Personal Toll

Confronting prejudice and discrimination took a personal toll on Sonja. The emotional labor involved in constantly battling societal norms and biases can lead to burnout and mental health challenges. Sonja often spoke about the anxiety and stress that accompanied her activism, particularly in the face of public backlash. The psychological impact of encountering prejudice is well-documented, with studies indicating that prolonged exposure can lead to feelings of isolation, depression, and diminished self-worth among activists.

Mental Health Impact $=$ Exposure to Prejudice $\times$ Duration of Activism

This equation illustrates the compounded effect of sustained exposure to discrimination on mental health, highlighting the need for support systems within activist communities.

Examples of Resistance

Sonja's efforts were not without resistance. In one notable instance, a proposed bill aimed at mandating LGBTQ-inclusive curricula in schools faced significant opposition from conservative groups who launched a campaign to discredit the initiative. Sonja, along with her allies, organized counter-protests and engaged in media campaigns to raise awareness about the benefits of inclusive education.

Furthermore, she utilized social media platforms to mobilize support, creating a digital space where allies could share their stories and experiences. This approach not only galvanized public support but also helped to counteract the negative narratives perpetuated by opposition groups.

Conclusion

Confronting prejudice and discrimination is an ongoing battle that requires resilience, creativity, and collaboration. Sonja Eggerickx's journey illustrates the multifaceted nature of activism and the importance of addressing both individual attitudes and systemic barriers. Through education, personal storytelling, coalition building, and advocacy, she has made significant strides in challenging prejudice, paving the way for a more inclusive society. The fight against discrimination is far from over, but the groundwork laid by activists like Sonja continues to inspire future generations to stand up for equality and justice.

The personal toll of activism

Activism, while a noble and essential pursuit, often comes with profound personal costs. For Sonja Eggerickx, the journey toward championing LGBTQ rights in

Belgium was not without its challenges, both emotionally and physically. The relentless nature of activism can lead to what is known as *activist burnout*, a state of emotional, physical, and mental exhaustion caused by prolonged and intense activism. This phenomenon is well-documented in the literature on social movements and can manifest in various ways, including chronic fatigue, anxiety, and feelings of helplessness (Maslach & Leiter, 2016).

Emotional Strain

The emotional toll of activism can be particularly taxing. Activists like Sonja often find themselves at the forefront of societal conflicts, facing backlash from those opposed to change. The constant exposure to hostility can lead to a sense of isolation. Research indicates that activists frequently endure a form of *moral distress*, where they feel compelled to act against injustices but are confronted with systemic barriers that hinder their efforts (Litz, 2009). For Sonja, this manifested as a struggle between her desire to advocate for LGBTQ rights and the societal pushback she encountered.

Moreover, the emotional weight of witnessing discrimination and violence against the LGBTQ community can lead to vicarious trauma. This term refers to the emotional duress experienced by individuals who are indirectly exposed to the suffering of others. Sonja often found herself grappling with the stories of LGBTQ youth facing bullying and rejection, which took a toll on her mental health. The cumulative effect of these experiences can create a pervasive sense of despair, making it difficult for activists to maintain their resolve.

Physical Exhaustion

In addition to emotional challenges, the physical demands of activism can be overwhelming. The need to attend countless meetings, protests, and community events often leads to a grueling schedule that leaves little time for self-care. Sonja's commitment to her cause often meant sacrificing her own well-being, leading to sleep deprivation and stress-related health issues. The concept of *self-care* is crucial in activism, as it allows individuals to recharge and sustain their efforts over time (Reed, 2015). However, many activists, including Sonja, struggle to prioritize their own needs amid the pressing demands of their work.

The physical toll can also extend to the risk of violence and harassment. Activists advocating for LGBTQ rights often face threats and intimidation from opposition groups. This not only creates a hostile environment but also instills a constant sense of fear. For Sonja, the knowledge that her activism could make her a target weighed heavily on her psyche, contributing to a heightened state of alertness that further exacerbated her stress levels.

Societal Isolation

The societal repercussions of activism can lead to a profound sense of isolation. Many activists find themselves alienated from friends, family, or community members who may not share their views. Sonja experienced this firsthand; as she became more vocal in her advocacy, she noticed a shift in her relationships. Some friends distanced themselves, unable to reconcile their beliefs with her activism. This isolation can lead to a lack of support systems, making it even more challenging to cope with the pressures of activism.

Research has shown that social support plays a critical role in mitigating the effects of stress (Cohen & Wills, 1985). However, for activists who face societal rejection, finding this support can be an uphill battle. Sonja had to actively seek out like-minded individuals within the LGBTQ community, which, while ultimately rewarding, required significant emotional labor.

Conclusion

In conclusion, the personal toll of activism is a multifaceted issue that encompasses emotional, physical, and societal dimensions. For Sonja Eggerickx, the fight for LGBTQ rights was a source of both empowerment and strain. Understanding the challenges faced by activists is essential for fostering a supportive environment that encourages resilience and sustainability in their efforts. As Sonja's journey illustrates, acknowledging and addressing the personal costs of activism is crucial for the longevity of the movement and the well-being of its advocates.

Building bridges with policymakers

Advocating for LGBTQ rights in legislation

Advocating for LGBTQ rights in legislation is a critical component of the broader struggle for equality and justice. This advocacy involves not only the formulation of laws that protect LGBTQ individuals but also the active engagement with policymakers to ensure that these laws are enacted and enforced. The process is often fraught with challenges, including societal resistance, political opposition, and the pervasive influence of discriminatory beliefs.

Theoretical Framework

The advocacy for LGBTQ rights can be understood through various theoretical lenses, including social justice theory, which posits that all individuals deserve equitable treatment and protection under the law. This theory emphasizes the importance of addressing systemic inequalities and the need for legislative measures that promote inclusivity. Additionally, the theory of intersectionality highlights how different aspects of identity—such as race, gender, and sexual orientation—intersect to shape an individual's experience of discrimination. This framework is essential for understanding the multifaceted nature of LGBTQ rights advocacy, as it calls for laws that are not only inclusive of sexual orientation but also consider the diverse experiences within the LGBTQ community.

Challenges in Legislative Advocacy

Advocating for LGBTQ rights in legislation presents several challenges. One significant issue is the existence of laws that perpetuate discrimination. For instance, in many jurisdictions, laws that criminalize same-sex relationships or deny marriage rights to same-sex couples have historically been prevalent. These laws create a hostile environment for LGBTQ individuals and hinder their ability to live freely and authentically.

Another challenge is the political landscape, which can be polarized regarding LGBTQ issues. Advocacy efforts often face opposition from conservative groups that seek to maintain traditional definitions of family and marriage. This opposition can manifest in the form of legislative proposals aimed at rolling back existing protections or preventing the introduction of new ones. For example, in 2015, the Australian government faced significant backlash from conservative factions when it considered legislation to legalize same-sex marriage, highlighting the contentious nature of LGBTQ rights advocacy.

Successful Legislative Advocacy Examples

Despite these challenges, there have been notable successes in LGBTQ legislative advocacy that serve as powerful examples of effective activism. One such example is the legalization of same-sex marriage in Belgium in 2003, making it one of the first countries in the world to do so. This landmark legislation was the result of years of advocacy by LGBTQ activists, who worked tirelessly to educate the public and lobby lawmakers. The success of this initiative was bolstered by widespread public support, which was cultivated through awareness campaigns that highlighted the importance of equality and the right to love.

Another significant achievement is the introduction of anti-discrimination laws that protect LGBTQ individuals in various aspects of life, including employment, housing, and healthcare. For instance, the Equality Act 2010 in the United Kingdom provides comprehensive protections against discrimination based on sexual orientation and gender identity, ensuring that LGBTQ individuals can live and work without fear of prejudice. This legislation was the culmination of extensive advocacy efforts, including grassroots mobilization, coalition-building with allied organizations, and strategic lobbying of lawmakers.

Strategies for Effective Advocacy

To effectively advocate for LGBTQ rights in legislation, activists employ a range of strategies. Grassroots mobilization is a key tactic, as it helps to build a broad base of support for LGBTQ issues. Organizing community events, rallies, and awareness campaigns can galvanize public opinion and put pressure on lawmakers to act.

Additionally, forming coalitions with other marginalized groups can enhance advocacy efforts. By highlighting the interconnectedness of various social justice issues, activists can create a unified front that demands comprehensive legislative change. For example, partnerships with racial justice organizations can help to address the unique challenges faced by LGBTQ individuals of color, ensuring that advocacy efforts are inclusive and representative of the community's diversity.

Engaging in direct lobbying of lawmakers is another crucial strategy. This involves meeting with legislators to present data, personal stories, and research that underscore the need for LGBTQ-inclusive policies. Advocacy groups often provide training for activists to effectively communicate their message and navigate the political landscape, ensuring that their voices are heard in legislative discussions.

Conclusion

In conclusion, advocating for LGBTQ rights in legislation is a vital aspect of the movement for equality. While challenges abound, the successes achieved through dedicated advocacy efforts demonstrate the power of activism in shaping a more inclusive society. By employing strategic approaches that leverage public support, coalition-building, and direct engagement with policymakers, LGBTQ activists can continue to drive legislative change that protects and uplifts the rights of all individuals, regardless of their sexual orientation or gender identity. The ongoing fight for LGBTQ rights in legislation is not just about legal recognition; it is about affirming the dignity and humanity of every individual, fostering a society where everyone can thrive without fear of discrimination.

Lobbying for LGBTQ-inclusive policies

Lobbying for LGBTQ-inclusive policies is a critical component of the broader struggle for equality and social justice. At its core, lobbying involves advocating for specific legislation or policy changes that can enhance the rights and protections of LGBTQ individuals. This section explores the theory behind effective lobbying, the challenges faced by activists, and notable examples of successful advocacy.

Theoretical Framework

The theoretical framework for lobbying can be understood through the lens of social movement theory, which posits that collective action can lead to significant social change. According to Tilly and Tarrow (2015), social movements are characterized by sustained campaigns of claim-making that employ a variety of tactics, including lobbying. Activists leverage their collective power to influence policymakers by presenting compelling arguments, data, and personal testimonies that highlight the need for LGBTQ-inclusive policies.

Identifying Key Issues

To effectively lobby for LGBTQ-inclusive policies, activists must first identify key issues that require legislative attention. These issues may include:

+ **Anti-discrimination laws:** Ensuring that LGBTQ individuals are protected from discrimination in employment, housing, and public accommodations.

+ **Marriage equality:** Advocating for the legal recognition of same-sex marriages and partnerships.

+ **Transgender rights:** Pushing for policies that affirm the rights of transgender individuals, including access to healthcare and legal recognition of gender identity.

+ **Youth protections:** Promoting policies that protect LGBTQ youth from bullying and discrimination in educational settings.

Challenges in Lobbying

Despite the importance of lobbying, activists often face significant challenges. These challenges can be categorized into three main areas:

1. **Societal Resistance:** Many policymakers may be hesitant to support LGBTQ-inclusive policies due to prevailing societal attitudes. For instance, in regions where conservative beliefs dominate, advocating for LGBTQ rights can be met with hostility and backlash.

2. **Institutional Barriers:** Legislative processes can be complex and slow-moving. Activists must navigate bureaucratic hurdles, which may include lengthy committee reviews and the need to build coalitions with other interest groups.

3. **Limited Resources:** Many LGBTQ organizations operate with limited funding and resources, making it difficult to mount extensive lobbying campaigns. This can hinder their ability to conduct research, mobilize supporters, and engage in sustained advocacy efforts.

Strategies for Effective Lobbying

To overcome these challenges, LGBTQ activists have employed various strategies in their lobbying efforts:

+ **Building Coalitions:** Forming alliances with other marginalized groups can amplify the voice of LGBTQ activists. For example, the coalition of LGBTQ organizations and women's rights groups has successfully lobbied for comprehensive anti-discrimination legislation in several countries.

+ **Utilizing Data and Research:** Presenting data that illustrates the negative impact of discrimination on LGBTQ individuals can be a powerful tool in lobbying efforts. Research studies showing the correlation between anti-LGBTQ policies and mental health issues among LGBTQ youth have been instrumental in advocating for policy change.

+ **Grassroots Mobilization:** Engaging the community through grassroots efforts can create a groundswell of support for LGBTQ-inclusive policies. Organizing rallies, petitions, and letter-writing campaigns can demonstrate to policymakers that there is significant public demand for change.

Notable Examples

Several notable examples illustrate the effectiveness of lobbying for LGBTQ-inclusive policies:

- **The Marriage Equality Movement:** In many countries, the push for marriage equality was driven by organized lobbying efforts. Activists shared personal stories, engaged in public campaigns, and lobbied legislators to recognize same-sex marriage. In 2015, the U.S. Supreme Court's decision in *Obergefell v. Hodges* was a landmark victory for LGBTQ rights, resulting from years of persistent lobbying and advocacy.

- **Transgender Rights Advocacy:** The successful passage of the Equality Act in various jurisdictions has been largely attributed to the tireless efforts of transgender rights activists who lobbied for comprehensive protections. Their work highlighted the unique challenges faced by transgender individuals, effectively swaying public opinion and garnering legislative support.

- **Educational Policy Changes:** In Belgium, activists successfully lobbied for the inclusion of LGBTQ topics in school curricula. This was achieved through collaboration with educational organizations, providing resources for teachers, and advocating for policy changes that promote inclusivity in education.

Conclusion

Lobbying for LGBTQ-inclusive policies is an essential aspect of the fight for equality. By understanding the theoretical underpinnings of advocacy, identifying key issues, and employing effective strategies, activists can overcome challenges and create meaningful change. The ongoing efforts to lobby for LGBTQ rights not only impact legislation but also shape societal attitudes, paving the way for a more inclusive future.

Influencing public opinion

Influencing public opinion is a critical aspect of LGBTQ activism, as it shapes societal attitudes and can lead to significant changes in policy and legislation. Public opinion acts as both a reflection of societal values and a catalyst for change, making it essential for activists like Sonja Eggerickx to engage with the community and reshape perceptions regarding LGBTQ issues.

Theoretical Framework

The influence of public opinion can be understood through several theoretical lenses, including the **Spiral of Silence Theory** and the **Framing Theory**. The

Spiral of Silence Theory, proposed by Elisabeth Noelle-Neumann, posits that individuals are less likely to express their opinions if they perceive themselves to be in the minority, leading to a self-reinforcing cycle of silence and marginalization. Conversely, Framing Theory, articulated by Erving Goffman, emphasizes how the presentation of information can shape perceptions and influence public discourse.

Challenges in Influencing Public Opinion

Despite the theoretical frameworks that guide activism, various challenges complicate the task of influencing public opinion. These challenges include:

- **Media Representation:** The portrayal of LGBTQ individuals in the media often oscillates between stereotypes and sensationalism, which can skew public perception. For instance, negative portrayals can reinforce prejudices, while positive representations can foster empathy and understanding.

- **Cultural Resistance:** In many societies, deeply entrenched cultural norms and values can create resistance to LGBTQ rights. Activists must navigate these cultural landscapes carefully, often facing backlash from conservative groups.

- **Misinformation:** The spread of misinformation regarding LGBTQ issues can lead to misconceptions that hinder progress. Addressing false narratives is crucial in shaping informed public opinion.

Strategies for Influencing Public Opinion

Sonja Eggerickx employed various strategies to influence public opinion effectively, including:

1. **Storytelling:** Personal narratives play a powerful role in humanizing LGBTQ issues. By sharing her own experiences and those of others, Sonja was able to foster empathy and understanding among diverse audiences. For example, during her speeches and public appearances, she often highlighted the struggles and triumphs of LGBTQ youth, making the issues relatable and urgent.

2. **Engaging with Media:** Collaborating with journalists and media outlets allowed Sonja to ensure that LGBTQ stories were told authentically and positively. By providing accurate information and expert commentary, she

helped shape media narratives to reflect the realities of the LGBTQ community.

3. **Utilizing Social Media:** In the digital age, social media has emerged as a powerful tool for activism. Sonja leveraged platforms like Twitter and Instagram to disseminate information, mobilize support, and engage with the public directly. Campaigns that went viral often led to increased awareness and support for LGBTQ rights.

4. **Public Campaigns:** Organizing public awareness campaigns, such as pride marches and educational workshops, helped Sonja create visible demonstrations of support for LGBTQ rights. These events not only raised awareness but also fostered community solidarity, encouraging individuals to publicly express their support.

Case Studies

Several case studies highlight the effectiveness of these strategies in influencing public opinion:

+ **The Marriage Equality Campaign:** In Belgium, the campaign for marriage equality saw a significant shift in public opinion over a decade. Through consistent advocacy, media engagement, and personal storytelling, activists like Sonja helped to change perceptions about same-sex relationships, culminating in the legalization of same-sex marriage in 2003. Polls indicated that support for marriage equality rose from 32% in 2001 to 70% by 2013, illustrating the power of sustained activism.

+ **Anti-Bullying Initiatives:** Sonja's efforts in advocating for anti-bullying policies in schools also contributed to changing attitudes towards LGBTQ youth. By partnering with educational institutions and sharing testimonials from affected students, she was able to raise awareness about the prevalence of bullying and its impact. Surveys conducted post-initiative showed a 40% decrease in reported bullying incidents in participating schools, indicating a shift in both policy and public sentiment.

Conclusion

In conclusion, influencing public opinion is a multifaceted endeavor that requires strategic engagement, resilience, and creativity. Sonja Eggerickx's work exemplifies how activists can navigate challenges and employ effective strategies to reshape societal attitudes towards LGBTQ rights. By fostering empathy through storytelling, engaging with media, utilizing social media, and organizing public campaigns, activists can create a ripple effect that ultimately leads to greater acceptance and equality. The ongoing struggle for LGBTQ rights hinges not only on legal reforms but also on the hearts and minds of the public, making the task of influencing opinion as critical as any legislative battle.

Chapter Five: Impact and Legacy

Positive outcomes of LGBTQ education

Empowering LGBTQ youth

Empowering LGBTQ youth is a critical aspect of fostering an inclusive and supportive environment that allows young individuals to thrive. The journey of empowerment begins with education, awareness, and the creation of safe spaces where LGBTQ youth can express their identities without fear of discrimination or violence.

Theoretical Framework

To understand the empowerment of LGBTQ youth, we can draw on several theoretical frameworks, including the Social Identity Theory and the Empowerment Theory. Social Identity Theory posits that individuals derive a sense of self from their group memberships, which is particularly pertinent for LGBTQ youth who may struggle with acceptance within their social circles. According to [?], individuals often categorize themselves and others into social groups, leading to a sense of belonging that can bolster self-esteem and identity affirmation.

Empowerment Theory, on the other hand, emphasizes the process through which individuals gain control over their lives and decisions. This theory is particularly relevant in the context of LGBTQ youth, who often face systemic barriers that limit their autonomy. Empowerment involves three key components: gaining access to resources, developing skills, and fostering a sense of agency [?].

Challenges Faced by LGBTQ Youth

Despite the progress made in LGBTQ rights, many young individuals continue to face significant challenges. A study by the *Trevor Project* found that LGBTQ youth are more than twice as likely to experience bullying in school compared to their heterosexual peers [?]. This bullying can take various forms, including verbal harassment, physical violence, and social exclusion, leading to detrimental effects on mental health.

Furthermore, the lack of LGBTQ-inclusive curricula in schools can perpetuate feelings of isolation and invisibility among LGBTQ youth. Research indicates that inclusive education not only benefits LGBTQ students but also promotes understanding and acceptance among their peers [?].

Programs and Initiatives for Empowerment

In response to these challenges, organizations and initiatives have emerged to empower LGBTQ youth. For instance, the *LGBTQ Education Foundation* has developed programs aimed at creating safe spaces within schools. These programs include training for educators on LGBTQ issues, providing resources for students, and establishing support groups that foster community and belonging.

One notable initiative is the *GSA Network*, which supports the formation of Gender and Sexuality Alliances (GSAs) in schools across the country. These student-led organizations work to create safe environments for LGBTQ youth, promote awareness, and advocate for inclusive policies. According to a study by [?], schools with GSAs report lower rates of bullying and higher levels of acceptance among students.

Real-World Impact

The impact of empowering LGBTQ youth is profound. Empowered individuals are more likely to engage in their communities, advocate for their rights, and support others facing similar challenges. For example, the *It Gets Better Project* has provided a platform for LGBTQ individuals to share their stories of resilience and hope, inspiring countless young people to embrace their identities.

Moreover, studies show that LGBTQ youth who have access to supportive environments and resources are less likely to experience mental health issues. According to [?], LGBTQ youth with supportive networks report lower levels of depression and anxiety, highlighting the importance of empowerment in promoting overall well-being.

Conclusion

In conclusion, empowering LGBTQ youth is not merely a matter of providing resources; it is about fostering a culture of acceptance, understanding, and support. By leveraging theoretical frameworks such as Social Identity Theory and Empowerment Theory, we can better understand the unique challenges faced by LGBTQ youth and the importance of creating inclusive environments. Initiatives like the LGBTQ Education Foundation and the GSA Network exemplify the positive impact of empowerment, illustrating that when LGBTQ youth are supported, they can thrive and become advocates for change in their communities.

Creating safer school environments

The establishment of safer school environments for LGBTQ youth is paramount in fostering a sense of belonging and acceptance. Research has consistently shown that inclusive educational settings significantly reduce the prevalence of bullying, harassment, and discrimination, which are all too common in traditional school environments. According to the *National School Climate Survey*, LGBTQ students often experience hostile school climates, which can lead to detrimental effects on their mental health, academic performance, and overall well-being.

Theoretical Framework

The theoretical underpinning for creating safer school environments can be explored through the lens of *Social Identity Theory* (Tajfel & Turner, 1979). This theory posits that individuals derive a sense of identity and self-esteem from their group memberships. For LGBTQ students, affirming their identity within the school context is crucial. When schools actively promote inclusivity, they not only validate LGBTQ identities but also foster a collective sense of belonging that enhances self-esteem and reduces feelings of isolation.

Identifying Problems

Despite the clear benefits of inclusive environments, many schools continue to grapple with significant challenges:

- **Bullying and Harassment:** LGBTQ students are at a higher risk of being bullied compared to their heterosexual peers. The *Gay, Lesbian and Straight Education Network (GLSEN)* reports that more than 60% of LGBTQ students feel unsafe at school due to their sexual orientation.

• **Lack of Awareness and Training:** Many educators lack the necessary training to address LGBTQ issues effectively. This gap can lead to unintentional reinforcement of stereotypes and biases, further alienating LGBTQ students.

• **Inadequate Policies:** Schools often lack comprehensive anti-bullying policies that specifically address LGBTQ-related incidents. This absence of clear guidelines can create an environment where discrimination is tolerated or overlooked.

Implementing Solutions

To combat these challenges and create safer school environments, several strategies can be employed:

1. **Comprehensive Training for Educators:** Professional development programs should be instituted to equip teachers with the knowledge and skills to support LGBTQ students. Training should include understanding gender identity, sexual orientation, and the specific challenges faced by LGBTQ youth.

2. **Inclusive Policies:** Schools must adopt and enforce policies that explicitly protect LGBTQ students from discrimination and harassment. This includes revising codes of conduct to include protections based on sexual orientation and gender identity.

3. **Safe Spaces and Support Groups:** Establishing Gay-Straight Alliances (GSAs) and other support groups can provide LGBTQ students with a safe haven where they can express themselves freely. These groups can also promote awareness and understanding among the broader student body.

4. **Curriculum Integration:** Integrating LGBTQ topics into the school curriculum can normalize discussions around diversity and inclusion. This can be achieved through literature, history, and social studies that reflect LGBTQ contributions and experiences.

Examples of Successful Initiatives

Several schools and districts have implemented successful initiatives aimed at creating safer environments for LGBTQ students:

+ The *LGBTQ+ Inclusive Schools Project:* This initiative, launched in various districts across the United States, focuses on training educators and staff on LGBTQ issues, developing inclusive curricula, and fostering collaboration with local LGBTQ organizations.

+ The *Safe Schools Coalition:* This coalition works with schools to develop resources and support systems specifically designed for LGBTQ students. Their comprehensive approach includes policy advocacy, training, and community engagement.

+ The *No Name-Calling Week:* An annual event that encourages students to speak out against name-calling and bullying, promoting a culture of respect and inclusion within schools. This initiative has successfully raised awareness and engaged students in discussions about diversity.

Conclusion

Creating safer school environments for LGBTQ youth is not merely a matter of policy but a fundamental human right. By addressing the systemic issues that contribute to unsafe school climates and implementing effective strategies, educators and administrators can cultivate spaces where all students feel valued and protected. As the research indicates, when LGBTQ students feel safe and supported, they are more likely to thrive academically and socially, paving the way for a more inclusive future for all.

$$\text{Safety Index} = \frac{\text{Supportive Policies} + \text{Inclusive Practices}}{\text{Bullying Incidents}} \tag{11}$$

This equation illustrates the relationship between supportive policies and practices and the frequency of bullying incidents. A higher Safety Index reflects a more conducive environment for LGBTQ students, underscoring the importance of proactive measures in education.

In conclusion, the journey toward creating safer school environments is ongoing, requiring continuous effort, commitment, and collaboration among all stakeholders in the educational community. By embracing inclusivity and advocating for LGBTQ rights, we can ensure that future generations of students can learn and grow in environments free from fear and discrimination.

Reducing LGBTQ-related bullying and violence

The reduction of LGBTQ-related bullying and violence in educational settings is a crucial aspect of fostering a safe and inclusive environment for all students. Research consistently shows that LGBTQ youth are disproportionately affected by bullying, harassment, and violence in schools, leading to severe emotional and psychological consequences. According to a study by the *Gay, Lesbian and Straight Education Network (GLSEN)* in their National School Climate Survey, LGBTQ students experience higher rates of victimization compared to their heterosexual peers, with nearly 60% reporting feeling unsafe at school due to their sexual orientation or gender identity.

Understanding the Problem

Bullying and violence against LGBTQ individuals often stem from deep-seated societal prejudices and misconceptions. Theories such as the *Social Identity Theory* suggest that individuals derive part of their identity from the groups to which they belong. When societal norms favor heterosexuality and cisgender identities, LGBTQ individuals may be viewed as outsiders, leading to stigmatization and discrimination. This can manifest in various forms of bullying, including verbal harassment, physical violence, and cyberbullying.

A significant problem lies in the lack of awareness and understanding among students and educators regarding LGBTQ issues. Many students may not have access to accurate information about sexual orientation and gender identity, perpetuating stereotypes and misinformation. For instance, a survey conducted by the *Pew Research Center* found that 40% of Americans believe that homosexuality should be discouraged by society, reflecting a broader societal bias that can infiltrate school environments.

The Role of Education in Reducing Violence

Education plays a pivotal role in combating LGBTQ-related bullying and violence. By implementing comprehensive LGBTQ-inclusive curriculums, schools can create an environment where diversity is celebrated, and all students feel valued. Research indicates that when students learn about LGBTQ history and contributions, they are more likely to develop empathy and understanding towards their peers.

One effective approach is the implementation of programs such as *Safe Zones*, which train educators and students to become allies for LGBTQ individuals. These programs often include workshops that address the specific challenges faced by LGBTQ youth, equipping participants with the tools needed to intervene when witnessing bullying or harassment. A study published in the *Journal of School Violence* found that schools with Safe Zone programs reported a significant decrease in bullying incidents, showcasing the effectiveness of education in fostering a supportive school climate.

Creating Supportive Policies

To further reduce LGBTQ-related bullying and violence, schools must establish clear anti-bullying policies that explicitly include protections for LGBTQ students. The *Equality Act*, for example, aims to prohibit discrimination based on sexual orientation and gender identity in various areas, including education. Such legislative measures are essential in creating a framework that supports LGBTQ youth and holds perpetrators accountable for their actions.

Moreover, schools should implement reporting mechanisms that allow students to safely report incidents of bullying without fear of retaliation. Research by the *Trevor Project* indicates that LGBTQ youth who feel supported by their school are 40% less likely to experience suicidal ideation. This highlights the importance of creating a culture of support and accountability within educational institutions.

Examples of Successful Initiatives

Several schools and organizations have successfully implemented programs aimed at reducing LGBTQ-related bullying and violence. For instance, the *It Gets Better Project* has inspired countless individuals to share their stories of resilience, helping to reduce feelings of isolation among LGBTQ youth. Similarly, the *Human Rights Campaign* has developed resources for schools to create inclusive environments, including guides on how to address bullying and promote acceptance.

In Belgium, the initiatives led by Sonja Eggerickx and the LGBTQ Education Foundation have been instrumental in creating safer school environments. By advocating for inclusive policies and providing educators with the resources they need, these efforts have resulted in a noticeable decline in bullying incidents reported by students. Schools that have adopted comprehensive LGBTQ education have reported not only a reduction in bullying but also an increase in overall student well-being.

Conclusion

Reducing LGBTQ-related bullying and violence in schools is a multifaceted challenge that requires a concerted effort from educators, policymakers, and communities. By fostering an inclusive educational environment through awareness, supportive policies, and effective programs, we can empower LGBTQ youth and create a culture of respect and acceptance. As we continue to advocate for LGBTQ rights, it is imperative to recognize that education is not just a tool for learning; it is a powerful catalyst for change that can transform lives and build a more equitable society for all.

Broadening the scope of activism

Extending LGBTQ education beyond schools

As the landscape of LGBTQ rights continues to evolve, the need for comprehensive education that extends beyond the walls of schools becomes increasingly evident. While schools serve as critical environments for fostering understanding and acceptance, the influence of societal norms and cultural attitudes often permeates far beyond educational institutions. To create a truly inclusive society, LGBTQ education must be integrated into various sectors, including community organizations, workplaces, and public spaces.

Theoretical Framework

To understand the necessity of extending LGBTQ education, we can draw upon the Social Learning Theory, which posits that individuals learn from one another through observation, imitation, and modeling. This theory underscores the importance of role models and the impact of societal attitudes on personal behavior. By incorporating LGBTQ education into diverse environments, we can create a culture of acceptance that encourages individuals to challenge stereotypes and foster inclusivity.

Moreover, the Critical Pedagogy framework emphasizes the role of education in promoting social justice and equity. By extending LGBTQ education beyond schools, we can engage in a broader dialogue about power dynamics and the systemic inequalities faced by marginalized communities. This approach not only empowers LGBTQ individuals but also educates allies, fostering a collective responsibility to advocate for change.

Challenges to Implementation

Despite the clear benefits of extending LGBTQ education, several challenges must be addressed. One significant barrier is the entrenched societal stigma surrounding LGBTQ issues. Many community organizations and workplaces may be hesitant to incorporate LGBTQ content due to fears of backlash or alienation of certain demographics. Additionally, a lack of resources and training for educators and facilitators can hinder the effective delivery of LGBTQ education in non-school settings.

Furthermore, cultural differences play a crucial role in how LGBTQ topics are perceived and discussed. In some communities, traditional values may conflict with progressive ideals, leading to resistance against LGBTQ education. It is essential to approach these challenges with sensitivity and a commitment to dialogue, recognizing that change often requires time and patience.

Examples of Successful Initiatives

Despite these challenges, numerous initiatives have successfully extended LGBTQ education beyond traditional educational settings. For instance, organizations like *PFLAG* (Parents, Families, and Friends of Lesbians and Gays) have developed programs that educate families and community members about LGBTQ issues. These programs often include workshops, support groups, and informational resources that empower individuals to become advocates for LGBTQ rights within their communities.

In the workplace, companies such as *Google* and *Salesforce* have implemented comprehensive diversity training programs that include LGBTQ education. These initiatives not only promote a culture of inclusivity but also enhance employee morale and productivity. Research has shown that diverse and inclusive workplaces lead to improved job satisfaction and lower turnover rates, highlighting the tangible benefits of extending LGBTQ education into professional environments.

Additionally, public spaces such as libraries and community centers have begun hosting LGBTQ-themed events and workshops. These initiatives serve as safe havens for individuals to learn and engage with LGBTQ topics, fostering a sense of community and belonging. For example, the *Queer Library* initiative in various cities has created spaces where LGBTQ literature and resources are accessible to all, promoting awareness and understanding in the broader community.

Conclusion

Extending LGBTQ education beyond schools is not merely an option; it is a necessity for fostering an inclusive society. By leveraging theoretical frameworks such as Social Learning Theory and Critical Pedagogy, we can create a comprehensive approach to LGBTQ education that addresses the challenges and barriers faced in various settings. Through successful initiatives and community engagement, we can cultivate a culture of acceptance and advocacy that empowers individuals to embrace diversity and fight for equality. The journey toward inclusivity is ongoing, but by expanding our efforts beyond schools, we take significant strides toward a more equitable world for all.

Partnering with international organizations

The global landscape of LGBTQ rights is complex and multifaceted, requiring the collaboration of diverse stakeholders to effect meaningful change. Sonja Eggerickx recognized early on that local activism, while crucial, could be significantly amplified through partnerships with international organizations. These alliances not only provided a broader platform for advocacy but also facilitated the sharing of resources, strategies, and best practices across borders.

Theoretical Framework

The partnership between local activists and international organizations can be understood through the lens of *transnational advocacy networks* (TANs). According to Keck and Sikkink (1998), TANs are characterized by their ability to connect local issues with global movements, thereby enhancing the visibility and impact of social justice campaigns. This framework emphasizes the importance of collaboration in addressing systemic injustices, as it allows activists to leverage international support to challenge oppressive structures within their own countries.

Identifying Problems

One of the primary challenges faced by LGBTQ activists in Belgium—and indeed worldwide—is the persistent stigma and discrimination that permeates societal attitudes. Despite progress in certain areas, many LGBTQ individuals continue to face harassment, violence, and exclusion. This reality is compounded by the lack of comprehensive data on LGBTQ issues, which hinders effective advocacy.

Moreover, the political landscape in Belgium presents its own set of challenges. While the country has made significant strides in LGBTQ rights, including the legalization of same-sex marriage, there remains a need for ongoing advocacy to protect these rights from potential rollback. Activists often find themselves in a precarious position, balancing the need for local engagement with the desire for international solidarity.

Examples of Successful Partnerships

Sonja's collaboration with international organizations has yielded numerous successes.   One notable example is her partnership with *ILGA-Europe* (the International Lesbian, Gay, Bisexual, Trans and Intersex Association), which has been instrumental in advocating for LGBTQ rights across Europe. Through this partnership, Sonja was able to participate in EU-level discussions, bringing attention to the unique challenges faced by LGBTQ youth in Belgium.

Another significant collaboration involved the *United Nations Free & Equal* campaign, which focuses on promoting LGBTQ rights globally. By aligning her efforts with this campaign, Sonja was able to amplify her message and connect with a wider audience. This partnership provided access to valuable resources, including educational materials and training programs aimed at fostering LGBTQ-inclusive environments in schools.

Building Capacity and Resources

Through these international partnerships, Sonja was able to build capacity within the LGBTQ Education Foundation. The exchange of knowledge and resources facilitated the development of comprehensive educational programs tailored to the needs of LGBTQ students. For instance, the foundation launched a series of workshops in collaboration with international experts, focusing on creating safe spaces in schools and addressing bullying.

Moreover, the partnership with international organizations allowed for the collection of data and research that informed advocacy efforts. By utilizing global studies on LGBTQ youth experiences, Sonja was able to present compelling evidence to policymakers, demonstrating the urgent need for LGBTQ-inclusive education.

Challenges of International Collaboration

Despite the successes, partnering with international organizations is not without its challenges. Cultural differences can lead to misunderstandings, and the priorities of international bodies may not always align with local needs. For instance, while some international organizations may focus on legal reforms, local activists like Sonja often prioritize grassroots education and community-building efforts.

Additionally, there is the risk of overshadowing local voices in the pursuit of global recognition. Sonja was acutely aware of this dynamic and made it a point to ensure that local narratives were at the forefront of her advocacy. This approach not only empowered the local community but also fostered a sense of ownership over the initiatives being implemented.

Conclusion

In conclusion, Sonja Eggerickx's strategic partnerships with international organizations have significantly broadened the scope of her activism. By leveraging the power of transnational advocacy networks, she has been able to address systemic issues facing LGBTQ individuals in Belgium while contributing to the global movement for equality. The challenges inherent in these collaborations serve as a reminder of the importance of maintaining a local focus, ensuring that the voices of those most affected by discrimination are heard and prioritized. Ultimately, Sonja's work exemplifies the potential of international partnerships to create lasting change in the fight for LGBTQ rights.

Leaving a lasting impact on Belgium's LGBTQ movement

The legacy of Sonja Eggerickx is not merely a collection of accomplishments; it represents a profound transformation within Belgium's LGBTQ movement that continues to resonate today. This impact can be understood through various theoretical frameworks, including social change theory, which posits that sustained activism can lead to systemic shifts in societal attitudes and policies. Eggerickx's work is a testament to this theory, illustrating how grassroots initiatives can catalyze broader societal change.

One of the primary challenges faced by LGBTQ activists in Belgium was the deeply entrenched societal norms that perpetuated discrimination and stigma. The historical context of LGBTQ rights in Belgium, particularly before the legalization of same-sex marriage in 2003, was fraught with legal and social obstacles. Eggerickx's activism emerged as a response to these systemic barriers, highlighting the necessity of creating inclusive educational environments as a foundational step towards equality.

In her efforts to establish the LGBTQ Education Foundation, Eggerickx recognized that education was a powerful tool for dismantling prejudice. The foundation's initiatives were rooted in the belief that inclusive curricula could reshape the perceptions of LGBTQ individuals among young people. Research supports this notion; studies have shown that schools implementing LGBTQ-inclusive education experience a reduction in bullying and discrimination. For instance, a survey conducted by the Belgian LGBTQ advocacy group, Çavaria, found that schools with comprehensive LGBTQ education reported a 30% decrease in incidents of bullying related to sexual orientation and gender identity.

Furthermore, Eggerickx's work extended beyond the confines of traditional education. By partnering with international organizations such as ILGA-Europe (International Lesbian, Gay, Bisexual, Trans and Intersex Association), she was able to amplify the voice of Belgium's LGBTQ community on a global stage. This collaboration not only brought international attention to local issues but also allowed for the sharing of best practices and strategies among activists across Europe. The exchange of ideas and resources facilitated a more robust and united front against discrimination, fostering a sense of solidarity within the LGBTQ movement.

In addition to educational reforms, Eggerickx's advocacy efforts significantly influenced policy changes at the governmental level. By engaging with policymakers and presenting empirical evidence on the benefits of LGBTQ-inclusive policies, she was able to advocate for legislative changes that would protect and promote the rights of LGBTQ individuals. For example, her lobbying efforts contributed to the introduction of anti-discrimination laws that explicitly included sexual orientation and gender identity as protected categories. This legal framework has been instrumental in providing recourse for individuals facing discrimination in various spheres, including employment, housing, and public services.

Moreover, Eggerickx's legacy is reflected in the next generation of activists who continue to build upon her work. Young leaders within the LGBTQ community have cited her as a source of inspiration, often referencing her courage and determination in the face of adversity. This intergenerational transfer of knowledge and motivation is crucial for the sustainability of the movement, ensuring that the fight for LGBTQ rights remains vibrant and relevant.

The impact of Sonja Eggerickx's work is also evident in the cultural shift that has occurred in Belgium regarding LGBTQ acceptance. Public attitudes have evolved significantly, with increasing visibility and representation of LGBTQ individuals in media, politics, and public life. This cultural change can be attributed, in part, to the groundwork laid by activists like Eggerickx, who challenged societal norms and advocated for a more inclusive society.

In conclusion, Sonja Eggerickx's contributions to Belgium's LGBTQ movement have left an indelible mark on both the educational landscape and the broader societal framework. By intertwining activism with education and policy advocacy, she has created a legacy that not only addresses immediate issues faced by the LGBTQ community but also lays the foundation for future progress. The ongoing fight for LGBTQ rights in Belgium is a testament to her vision and determination, proving that the impact of one individual's efforts can resonate through generations, inspiring others to continue the struggle for equality and justice.

Conclusion

Sonja Eggerickx: A catalyst for change

Inspiring future generations of activists

The legacy of Sonja Eggerickx is not merely a reflection of her achievements; it is a beacon that illuminates the path for future generations of activists. Activism, particularly in the realm of LGBTQ rights, requires a blend of courage, resilience, and creativity. Eggerickx's journey exemplifies how one individual's commitment can galvanize a movement, inspiring countless others to join the fight for equality.

The Ripple Effect of Activism

Sonja's work has catalyzed a ripple effect, wherein her advocacy has empowered young activists to embrace their identities and champion LGBTQ rights. The concept of the *ripple effect* in activism can be understood through the lens of social learning theory, which posits that individuals learn from observing the behaviors of others, particularly role models. Bandura's (1977) social learning theory emphasizes that when individuals witness someone successfully advocating for change, they are more likely to engage in similar behaviors themselves.

For instance, Eggerickx's public coming out and her candid discussions about her experiences with discrimination have provided a framework for young LGBTQ individuals grappling with their own identities. By sharing her story, she has fostered an environment where others feel safe to express their truths, thus encouraging a new generation of activists to rise.

Empowerment through Education

Education plays a pivotal role in inspiring activism. Eggerickx's founding of the LGBTQ Education Foundation is a testament to her belief that knowledge equips individuals with the tools necessary to effect change. By developing comprehensive educational resources, she has not only informed students about LGBTQ issues but has also provided them with the confidence to advocate for themselves and others.

Research indicates that inclusive curricula significantly reduce feelings of isolation among LGBTQ youth, thereby increasing their likelihood of engaging in activism (Kosciw et al., 2018). This educational empowerment creates a cycle of advocacy where informed individuals become advocates, who in turn educate others, perpetuating a culture of activism.

Cultivating Community and Solidarity

Sonja's efforts have also emphasized the importance of community in activism. The LGBTQ community thrives on solidarity, and Eggerickx has worked tirelessly to foster connections among activists. The formation of alliances with other marginalized groups highlights the intersectionality of social justice movements.

Intersectionality, as articulated by Crenshaw (1989), posits that individuals experience multiple, overlapping identities that shape their experiences of oppression. By recognizing and addressing these intersections, Eggerickx has inspired future activists to adopt a more holistic approach to advocacy. This inclusivity not only strengthens the movement but also ensures that the voices of the most marginalized are heard.

Mentorship and Leadership Development

Mentorship is another critical component of inspiring future activists. Eggerickx has actively engaged in mentorship programs, guiding young activists as they navigate the complexities of advocacy. This mentorship not only provides practical skills but also instills a sense of purpose and belonging.

The importance of mentorship in activism is supported by the theory of *transformational leadership*, which emphasizes the role of leaders in inspiring and motivating followers to achieve their potential (Bass, 1985). By embodying the principles of transformational leadership, Eggerickx has fostered a new generation of leaders who are equipped to tackle the challenges of the LGBTQ rights movement.

Challenges and Resilience

Despite the progress made, future generations of activists will undoubtedly face challenges similar to those encountered by Eggerickx. The persistence of homophobia, transphobia, and institutional discrimination remains a significant barrier to achieving equality. However, Eggerickx's resilience serves as a powerful reminder that perseverance is key in the face of adversity.

The concept of *grit*, as defined by Duckworth (2007), underscores the importance of passion and perseverance in achieving long-term goals. By demonstrating grit in her activism, Eggerickx inspires future activists to remain steadfast in their pursuit of justice, even when the path is fraught with obstacles.

Conclusion: A Legacy of Inspiration

In conclusion, Sonja Eggerickx's impact on future generations of activists is profound and multifaceted. Through her commitment to education, community building, mentorship, and resilience, she has laid a foundation upon which future activists can build. The ongoing fight for LGBTQ rights requires not only the courage to confront injustice but also the inspiration to dream of a more inclusive world. As Eggerickx continues to inspire, she embodies the essence of activism: a relentless pursuit of equality that transcends generations.

The significance of inclusive education

Inclusive education is a crucial component of fostering a society that values diversity and promotes equality for all individuals, particularly those who identify as LGBTQ. The significance of inclusive education lies not only in its ability to provide a safe and supportive environment for LGBTQ youth but also in its potential to challenge societal norms, reduce stigma, and cultivate empathy among students. This section explores the theoretical foundations of inclusive education, the problems it aims to address, and real-world examples that illustrate its importance.

Theoretical Foundations

Inclusive education is grounded in several key theories that emphasize the importance of diversity, social justice, and human rights. One prominent theory is the *Social Model of Disability*, which posits that disability is not an individual deficiency but rather a result of societal barriers that exclude certain groups. This model can be extended to LGBTQ identities, highlighting how societal norms around gender and sexuality can marginalize individuals. By fostering an inclusive educational environment, schools can dismantle these barriers and promote understanding and acceptance.

Another significant theoretical framework is *Critical Pedagogy*, which encourages educators to question and challenge the status quo. This approach advocates for an educational system that empowers students to recognize and confront injustices, including those faced by LGBTQ individuals. By integrating LGBTQ topics into the curriculum, educators can stimulate critical discussions that promote awareness and understanding, ultimately leading to a more inclusive society.

Problems Addressed by Inclusive Education

The absence of inclusive education can lead to a myriad of problems for LGBTQ youth. One of the most pressing issues is the prevalence of bullying and harassment in schools. According to a study by the Gay, Lesbian and Straight Education Network (GLSEN), LGBTQ students are significantly more likely to experience bullying compared to their heterosexual peers. This not only affects their mental health but can also lead to academic underachievement and increased dropout rates.

Moreover, the lack of representation in the curriculum can result in feelings of isolation and invisibility among LGBTQ students. When their identities are not acknowledged or validated, it can perpetuate a sense of shame and contribute to mental health issues such as anxiety and depression. According to the Trevor Project, LGBTQ youth are more than twice as likely to experience suicidal ideation compared to their non-LGBTQ peers, underscoring the urgent need for inclusive educational practices.

Examples of Inclusive Education in Action

Real-world examples demonstrate the positive impact of inclusive education on LGBTQ youth. One notable initiative is the *LGBTQ+ Inclusive Curriculum Project* in the United Kingdom, which aims to integrate LGBTQ history and contributions into the national curriculum. By educating students about influential LGBTQ figures and events, the project fosters a more comprehensive understanding of history and promotes acceptance among students. Schools that have implemented this curriculum have reported a decrease in bullying incidents and an increase in student engagement.

In Belgium, the *LGBTQ Education Foundation*, founded by Sonja Eggerickx, serves as a model for inclusive education. The foundation provides resources and training for educators to create LGBTQ-inclusive classrooms. By developing comprehensive educational materials and facilitating workshops, the foundation empowers teachers to address LGBTQ issues effectively. As a result, students report feeling safer and more supported in their learning environments.

Conclusion

The significance of inclusive education cannot be overstated. It plays a vital role in creating safe spaces for LGBTQ youth, fostering empathy and understanding among students, and challenging societal norms that perpetuate discrimination. By addressing the problems faced by LGBTQ individuals in educational settings and implementing inclusive practices, we can pave the way for a more equitable society. As Sonja Eggerickx's work illustrates, inclusive education is not just a theoretical ideal; it is a necessary foundation for a future where all individuals, regardless of their sexual orientation or gender identity, can thrive.

The ongoing fight for LGBTQ rights and equality

The struggle for LGBTQ rights and equality is far from over, as the landscape of societal acceptance and legal recognition continues to evolve. While significant strides have been made in many parts of the world, including Belgium, where Sonja Eggerickx has been a pivotal figure, numerous challenges remain that activists must confront. This section explores the persistent issues faced by the LGBTQ community, the theoretical frameworks that inform contemporary activism, and the examples of ongoing efforts to secure equality.

Theoretical Frameworks in LGBTQ Activism

Understanding the ongoing fight for LGBTQ rights requires an examination of various theoretical frameworks that inform activism. One such framework is **intersectionality**, coined by Kimberlé Crenshaw, which emphasizes how different forms of discrimination—such as those based on race, gender, and sexual orientation—intersect to create unique experiences of oppression. This theory is crucial for LGBTQ activism as it highlights the necessity of addressing the diverse needs of individuals within the community, recognizing that not all experiences are the same.

Another important concept is **queer theory**, which challenges the binary understanding of gender and sexuality. Queer theory posits that identities are fluid and socially constructed, urging activists to advocate for a broader understanding of what it means to be LGBTQ. This theoretical lens encourages inclusivity and recognizes the spectrum of identities, thereby fostering a more comprehensive approach to rights advocacy.

Current Challenges

Despite advancements, the LGBTQ community still faces significant hurdles. One prominent issue is **discrimination and violence.** According to the International Lesbian, Gay, Bisexual, Trans and Intersex Association (ILGA), many LGBTQ individuals experience harassment, violence, and discrimination in various aspects of life, including employment, housing, and healthcare. For instance, reports indicate that transgender individuals, particularly transgender women of color, are disproportionately affected by violence, highlighting the urgent need for protective legislation.

Additionally, **conversion therapy** remains a contentious issue in many regions. This practice, which seeks to change an individual's sexual orientation or gender identity, is widely discredited by medical professionals but continues to be legal in several countries. Activists are working tirelessly to ban conversion therapy, advocating for mental health support that affirms rather than attempts to change LGBTQ identities.

Global Perspectives and Local Actions

The fight for LGBTQ rights is also marked by **global disparities.** In some countries, LGBTQ individuals face criminalization, persecution, and even death. For example, in regions where anti-LGBTQ laws are enforced, such as parts of Africa and the Middle East, activists risk their lives to fight for basic human rights. Organizations like Amnesty International and Human Rights Campaign work internationally to bring attention to these abuses and support local activists.

On a local level, grassroots movements continue to play a critical role in advocating for LGBTQ rights. In Belgium, activists build on the foundation laid by pioneers like Sonja Eggerickx by organizing community events, educational workshops, and awareness campaigns. These initiatives aim to foster understanding and acceptance, particularly among youth, who are often the most vulnerable to bullying and discrimination.

Examples of Ongoing Advocacy

One notable example of ongoing advocacy is the push for **inclusive education** in schools, which aims to create safe and affirming environments for LGBTQ students. Initiatives like the "Safe Schools" program in Australia have been instrumental in providing resources and training for educators to address LGBTQ issues in the classroom. By fostering an inclusive curriculum, these programs not only empower LGBTQ youth but also educate their peers, promoting a culture of respect and understanding.

Moreover, the fight for **marriage equality** and family rights continues in various parts of the world. Activists are advocating for legal recognition of same-sex partnerships and the right to adopt children, emphasizing that love and commitment should not be restricted by gender. The success of marriage equality in countries like Belgium serves as a beacon of hope, inspiring activists globally to pursue similar legal reforms.

Conclusion

In conclusion, the ongoing fight for LGBTQ rights and equality is a multifaceted struggle that requires a deep understanding of theoretical frameworks, acknowledgment of persistent challenges, and commitment to grassroots activism. As Sonja Eggerickx has demonstrated through her work, the journey towards equality is not only about securing legal rights but also about fostering a culture of acceptance and understanding. The ongoing efforts of activists around the world remind us that while progress has been made, the fight for LGBTQ rights is far from over. It is a call to action for current and future generations to continue advocating for a world where everyone, regardless of their sexual orientation or gender identity, can live freely and authentically.

$$\text{Activism} = \text{Awareness} + \text{Education} + \text{Community Engagement} \qquad (12)$$

Index

Milton Keynes UK
Ingram Content Group UK Ltd.
UKHW020320021124
450424UK00013B/1349

9 781779 697042